Barbie™

Her Inspiration, History, and Legacy

Barbie™

Her Inspiration, History, and Legacy

ROBIN GERBER

EPIC INK

This edition published in 2024 by Epic Ink, an imprint of The Quarto Group, 142 West 36th Street, 4th Floor, New York, NY 10018 USA (212) 779-4972 www.Quarto.com

First published in 2019 by by Epic Ink, an imprint of The Quarto Group, 1120 NE 33rd Place, Suite 201, Bellevue, Washington 98004.

The views, information, or opinions expressed herein are solely those of the individuals involved and do not necessarily represent those of the publisher, Mattel, Inc., or their respective employees.

10 9 8 7 6 5 4 3

ISBN: 978-0-7603-9122-8

Library of Congress Control Number: 2023950891

Group Publisher: Rage Kindelsperger
Creative Director: Laura Drew
Editorial Director: Lori Burke
Managing Editor: Cara Donaldson
Editors: Bonnie Honeycutt and Stacia Deutsch
Cover Design: Laura Drew
Interior Design: Megan Sugiyama
Text: Robin Gerber

Printed in China

CONTENTS

INTRODUCTION

Although I wrote the biography of Ruth Handler, entitled *Barbie and Ruth*, I would not have called myself a Barbie expert when I received the request. What interested me most about Barbie was her creator, an entrepreneurial genius and pioneering woman who co-founded the biggest toy company in the world: Mattel. Ruth's high concept—that little girls want to play at being big girls—fascinated me, and this book gave me the chance to answer some of the questions that had trailed me since writing Ruth's biography: How has Barbie lasted this long? And how long could she go on?

My journey led to Mattel headquarters in El Segundo, California, and the Barbie brand staff. In the enormous space, now decorated with the wild and rich imagination of an army of creators, I learned about who Barbie is today.

As the designers, artists, marketers, and managers explained Barbie, I kept thinking to myself, "Ruth would be so pleased." Her doll is being designed and promoted just as she intended, as a vehicle for a child to pretend to be anything. Ruth would appreciate the emphasis on diversity and inclusion. Because Ruth, and her husband Elliot

Handler, were Jewish, and had personal experience with anti-Semitism, they pushed back against discrimination in all forms. In fact, Ruth and Elliot were honored by the Urban League for their inclusive workforce.

I also had the chance to interview collectors and fans who live their personal creativity through the doll. You'll read about the man from Singapore who makes the most extraordinary Barbie clothes from tissue paper, and the young Australian girl who is a YouTube sensation for her live-action Barbie stories.

Ruth never imagined that Barbie would spark the imagination of all sorts of creators. Her genius was understanding the dreams of childhood. Dreams that we all carry into adult life, hoping to have them come true one day. I don't remember if I ever pretended that Barbie was a writer, but I always believed I could be anything. Perhaps Ruth's doll had something to do with that.

—Robin Gerber
Author

OPPOSITE: Mattel's 65th Anniversary dolls.

chapter 1

INSPIRING FANS SINCE 1959

There are endless ways to play with Barbie, and for decades, girls have loved the fantasies that the doll helps them create. Barbie lets them see themselves as women of action, women in the world doing interesting jobs and having amazing adventures. Girls see her as a blank slate that can reflect and embody their ideas about growing up.

Barbie sparks inspiration because her creator, Ruth Handler, embodied it herself. In a 1994 book titled *The Story of Barbie*, author Kitturah Westenhouser asked this thought-provoking question:

"Is it the doll or her mother, Ruth Handler, who is *really* the legend?"

Initially, Ruth wasn't known as a toy designer. When she and her husband, Elliot, along with their friend Harold Matson, began their company, Ruth ran operations as executive vice president. Mattel was established in January 1945, using Matson's last name combined with Elliot's first, but Ruth didn't complain at being left out of the name. She was happy behind the scenes marketing and managing the young toy business.

Every day, Ruth made hundreds of decisions that kept Mattel growing. She hired employees, inspected products, approved budgets, all while nurturing her family at home. Her life left little time for dreaming up new inventions, and yet, when "Barbie" flashed into her mind, Ruth had a strong feeling the doll would be popular. At the time, there was no way for her to know just how famous Barbie would become.

OPPOSITE: Barbie creator Ruth Handler in the 1960s. **FOLLOWING**: Mattel Creations, which was incorporated in 1948, located in Culver City, California. Their office would later move to a larger location in Hawthorne, California.

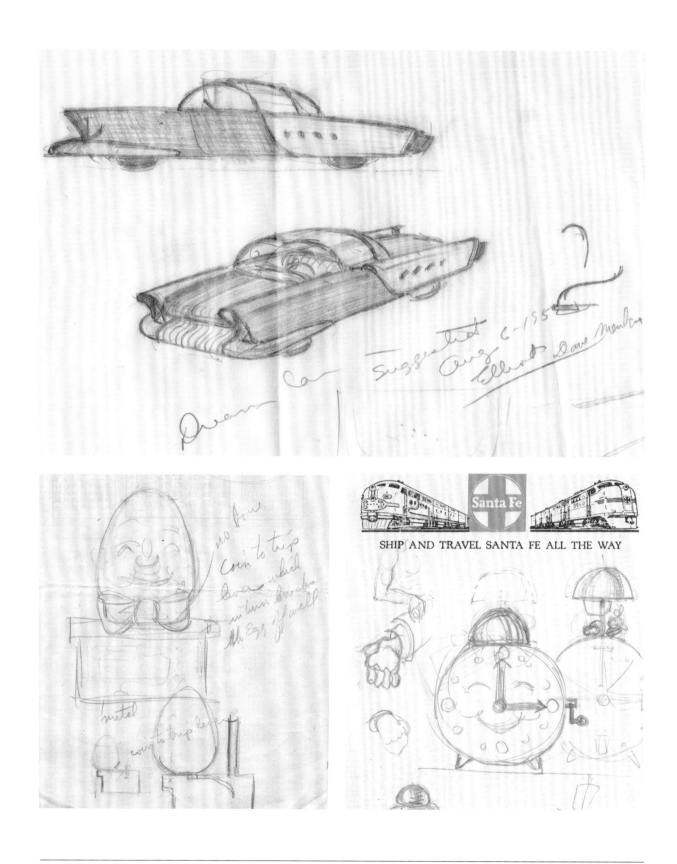

ABOVE: Original sketches from the 1950s by Elliot Handler, who was known to draft ideas on scratch paper, napkins, note paper, and anything he could use. Shown here are ideas for a Dream Car (top), Humpty Dumpty Rocker (bottom left), and the Hickory Dickory Clock (bottom right).

World War II ended in 1945. Soldiers were returning home and eagerly starting families. Americans' standard of living was rising. Families had more money, and more leisure time to spend it.

It was a perfect time to start a toy company.

Ruth had a terrific partner in her husband, Elliot. They'd met as teenagers in Denver, Colorado, and had been together ever since.

The toys that launched Mattel came from Elliot's fertile imagination and his skill at design. "You have to be able to spot trends," Ruth told a reporter in 1957. "My husband has a sixth sense. He's a great idea man." Research and design was Elliot's side, and since the first year when Harold Matson left

the business, Ruth handled everything else. She and Elliot had offices next to each other. People said there was "magic between them," both personally and in their work.

Mattel's first big hit was a miniature ukulele, called the Uke-a-Doodle, which came to market in 1947. Elliot had designed it to look like the ukulele played by Arthur Godfrey, a popular radio and television star. The original Uke-a-Doodle was made of plastic. It had steel strings and tunable pegs. In 1949, Elliot upgraded the Uke-a-Doodle by adding a small box with tiny wires that were plucked when a crank was turned. The toys would play a variety of short tunes.

Over the next few years, the music mechanism was put inside many other toys, including books. Within two years, music box toys brought in nearly nine million dollars.

Throughout the 1950s, Mattel came out with the Mousegetar, the Musical Egg, the Musical Clock, a Bonneville racing car, Jack and Popeye-in-the-Box, and more.

LEFT: Ruth and Elliot Handler in 1941, with newborn daughter Barbara at five-and-a-half weeks old. **RIGHT**: An advertisement from the 1948 Mattel Creations catalog for the Uke-a-Doodle Music Box, which was two toys in one: a child-size ukulele that also came with a music box that played popular tunes with the turn of its handle.

Chromatically tuned with real jet black keys that actually play

Futurland GRAND

Dimensions
Width: 8½ inches
Length: 11½ inches
Height Overall: 7¼ inches

Attractions:

★ 17 Plastic keys
★ Real sharps and flats
★ Chromatically tuned
★ New type, patented Sound Board
★ Feather touch action
★ Colorful two-tone variegated plastic

An all-year musical toy favorite . . . the musical toy with 17 plastic keys, 10 white and 7 jet black keys that actually play . . . the only table model toy piano that has sharps and flats. Fabricated of sturdy washable molded plastic in bright toy-tested colors . . . Futurland toys have always been leaders in sales, profits and consumer acceptance. Amazingly low priced for volume turnover.

Write for prices and information

No. 412 . . . Packed 1 dozen to a carton. Shipping weight 29 lbs. per carton. Terms: 2% 10 days E. O. M., F. O. B. Culver City. Regular trade discounts. Newspaper mats available.

Elliot's passion was "cowboy stuff" and riding horses. He enjoyed going to the desert, chasing coyotes on horseback, and taking the family to dude ranches, so toy guns were a natural extension of his personal interests. The musical toys set the standard, but the cowboy-themed products carried Mattel into even greater success.

From the earliest days, Mattel created doll furniture. Unlike that of their competitors, Mattel's furniture had hand-rubbed finishes and decorator upholstery fabric. The company made beautiful furniture, but no dolls. Soon, that would change.

During the war, women took all kinds of jobs, but when the soldiers came back, many of these women returned home to run their households and raise their children.

Little girls were given baby dolls so they could imitate what they saw in their own homes: cloth diapers that went in diaper pails for later cleaning, glass baby bottles that needed thorough sanitizing, and laundry sets that included gear for line drying.

TOP: Ruth and Elliot Handler in 1951 modeling some of their popular toys. **BOTTOM:** An advertisement from the 1951 Mattel Creations catalog for the Futurland Grand Piano.

ABOVE: Ruth Handler watches as her husband and founder of Mattel, Elliot Handler, interacts with the popular Jack-in-the-Box toy, in the 1960s.

ABOVE: The Handler family in the 1960s. (L-R) Kenneth, Elliot, Ruth, and Barbara.

Ruth realized something other toy makers had missed. In addition to the baby dolls, Ruth's daughter, Barbara, also loved playing with paper dolls. Girls could play at being adults or teens with these cutouts. They could act out roles, and they could pretend in a way that was impractical with baby dolls.

Barbara particularly liked color cutouts of Tillie the Toiler. Tillie had several fashionable outfits in her paper wardrobe. There were paper dolls of Hollywood stars like Elizabeth Taylor and Debbie Reynolds. Bridal party, colonial, and comic-book character dolls stuffed the dime-store shelves.

Paper dolls were simply cardboard images of women, often in underwear or a bathing suit, ready to be dressed. These dolls had to be carefully popped out of their backgrounds, which could then be stood up in a cardboard stand. They came with pages of clothes that needed to be tediously cut out with scissors. Tabs jutted out so that they could be folded and pressed down around the figures to stay on; however, the tabs worked poorly. Clothes rarely attached properly, and to add to the frustration, the tabs would often tear off, and then, the paper garments wouldn't work at all.

Still, Barbara and her friends preferred the paper dolls to the three-dimensional baby dolls on the market, such as Madame Alexander, Posie, and Dollikin. Madame Alexander dolls wore elaborate dresses and were treated more as collectibles than dolls made for active play. Dollikin might wear a fur stole and pearl earrings, but she still looked prepubescent.

As she watched her daughter playing with her friends, Ruth considered that paper dolls were an unrealistic hybrid between babies and teens. She noticed that girls were searching for a way to imitate the reality they observed in the adult world. Ruth wondered, *How much richer would their play be if the doll they held was three-dimensional, with adult clothes on an adult figure?*

"I decided," Ruth told *Good Housekeeping* in 1967, "that a doll with a teenage figure and lots of glorious, imaginative high-fashion clothes would be radically different, and would appeal to today's girls who grew up faster than they used to." Her characteristic optimism ensured her that it would sell. "My whole philosophy was that through this doll, girls could be anything they wanted to be." Ruth took her toy idea to Elliot, who always believed in her. But this time, Elliot pushed back.

The twenty male engineers at Mattel all agreed on one thing: mothers would never buy their daughters an adult doll with full-grown breasts. The men wanted to stay focused on the hot market of guns and rockets.

Guns and rockets were so popular in the mid-1950s that Mattel took a huge risk by advertising them on television, a relatively new medium for promoting toys. Ruth saw opportunity in gearing the ads directly toward children. Her strategy paid off when the Burp Gun advertisements aired on the new hit television show: *The Mickey Mouse Club.*

ABOVE: An example of popular paper dolls of the time, Mopsy Modes paper dolls were modeled after the *Mopsy* comic strip, created in 1939 by Gladys Parker, who was both a cartoonist and fashion designer. Gladys was able to expand her interest in fashion with concepts she created in a series of paper dolls.

ABOVE: Vintage illustration of High School Paper Dolls from 1940, first published by Merrill Publishing. Paper dolls and their interchangeable fashions were an inspiration in the creation of Barbie.

The Burp Gun, named for the sound of its bursting caps, was so widely popular that the team at Mattel overwhelmingly agreed that dolls were a risky distraction.

For Ruth, the men's attitudes were not roadblocks, but instead, drove her passion further. She was sure she would find a way to make her doll.

This was not the first time that Ruth had been told she couldn't do what she had in mind. Sarah, Ruth's older sister had tried to stop Ruth from marrying Elliot. After two years, Sarah finally gave up. Ruth was the kind of person whose determination grew when her dreams were denied. Just as she had persevered to marry Elliot, she held on to her doll idea, believing she could make it work.

Meanwhile, thousands of miles away, in Germany, Reinhard Beuthien—a tall square-jawed man with a twinkle in his eye and a cigarette dangling from his lips—had just created a hit cartoon. Beuthien worked for a tabloid newspaper, *Bild-Zeitung*, which means "picture." The editor asked Beuthien to come up with a cartoon to fill a space where a column had been pulled. Beuthien's first attempt featured a cherubic baby,

but when his editor balked, Beuthien put the baby face onto the voluptuous body of a young woman and called her Lilli.

The reaction to Lilli was enthusiastic. She was a hit across Germany. Taking advantage of his cartoon character's popularity, Beuthien teamed up with a toy designer to move Lilli off the page and to shape her into a three-dimensional doll. Although it was designed for adults, toy stores soon began carrying the buxom doll dressed in costumes ranging from a ski outfit to evening wear. As Ruth made plans for her family's first trip abroad, she had no idea that Lilli awaited her.

In July, 1956, Ruth and her family headed for a six-week tour of Europe aboard the great transatlantic cruise ship Queen Mary. It had been several years since Ruth first proposed her doll. She had made many efforts to interest her toy designers, patiently explaining her vision of an adult doll with tasteful makeup, nail polish, hair that could be styled, and realistic, well-made clothes. She was certain that Mattel could break new ground in the industry.

Even if the doll might sell, her engineers thought that the necessary plastic molding couldn't work. Nothing like she

---

ABOVE: Walt Disney (center) with Ruth and Elliot Handler, and several members of the Disney team, circa 1960.

described had ever been made, and certainly, it would cost too much to create.

In an interview with author Kitturah Westenhouser for her book, *The Story of Barbie*, Ruth explained that after touring London and Paris, the Handlers stopped at the Grand National Hotel in Lucerne, Switzerland. The palatial hotel, on the banks of Lake Lucerne, was magical. More magical still was the surprise awaiting Ruth when she went shopping with Barbara. Approaching a local shop, they looked in the window and found Lilli. She captivated them both, but for different reasons.

While Barbara was surprised to see that Lilli looked like a realistic version of her adult paper dolls, Ruth suddenly knew that the doll she envisioned *could* be manufactured, including its tiny details.

Ruth bought two Lilli dolls, one for herself and one for Barbara. She asked about clothing to go with them, but Lilli wasn't sold with separate clothes. If you wanted a different outfit, you had to buy another doll. Ruth concluded that if children bought one doll, they would buy clothing to dress it.

ABOVE: Ruth Handler assists Elliot assembling a two-stage plastic rocket next to a Number One Barbie.

Back at Mattel, Ruth showed the doll to their head of research and development, Jack Ryan, and to their production head, Seymour Adler.

In Lilli, Ruth had found a close approximation of the doll she had been describing, and she asked Jack to figure out how to make an original design. She estimated it would take about three years to get the doll to market.

Soon after, Jack was on his way to Japan to work on contracts for other toys, including wooden doll furniture that Elliot was designing. The planned furniture was for dolls two to three inches smaller than the 11½-inch doll that Ruth imagined. Ruth put Lilli in Jack's hands, so that they could also build larger furniture. She knew the design team would be winging it, since there wasn't a doll yet, but making a toy always entailed risk.

Mattel was just starting to manufacture in Japan because of lower labor costs. Ruth understood that to make her doll marketable, she would need the savings that could be found overseas. Ruth tapped Frank Nakamura to figure out how to make the doll itself.

ABOVE: Mattel designer Jack Ryan stands in front of a Fanner 50 display, circa 1957.

ABOVE: The cover of Mattel's Fall 1957 catalog featuring the Fanner 50.

ABOVE: Shown here in a blue dress with white polka dots is a 1955 Lilli doll from Germany.

Even though he spoke Japanese, Frank struggled to explain the doll's details to Japanese companies. Prototypes came out with different faces than Ruth intended, and with far too realistic-looking breasts. The prototypes were sent back to Mattel headquarters, some of the rejects ending up in desk drawers.

The Japanese engineers had their own problems. They labored to adjust the plastic molding so that every crevice was filled with the melted vinyl. If it wasn't perfect, the doll would come out of the mold with no nose, odd bubbles on the body, or with brittle fingers that broke off.

The first stands for the doll were also an issue. The original dolls had holes at the bottoms of the feet and shoes that fit over metal prongs at the bottom of the stand. The fit had to be exact or the doll would fall over. If the doll was pressed down too hard, a leg would break off. Costly inspections were required. The first stand was abandoned in favor of a wire rack stand, then later replaced with a stand

ABOVE: Designers are hard at work at the Mattel headquarters, circa 1960s.

that held the doll under the arms. All of these decisions had to be considered while determining the price. Ruth wanted to keep the price low, knowing that she was selling a tiny mannequin whose clothing and accessories would bring the greatest financial reward.

Ruth set out to find the best fashion designer in Los Angeles. She wanted someone who loved color, pattern, and material. They had to be precise, a perfectionist. Ruth—always aiming high—imagined realistic clothing right down to the snaps, buttons, belts, and zippers. Girls should feel like they were dressing a tiny person, a miniature embodiment of their future selves. A tiny purse, a pearl headband, shoes, sandals, boots, sunglasses with tinted lenses, hats with a hint of a veil—all these would hold children's attention and stimulate play.

Ruth found Charlotte Johnson at a social event. Charlotte had been a clothing designer on New York's Seventh Avenue. When Ruth met her, Charlotte was teaching clothing design at the famed Chouinard Art Institute, where Walt Disney sent animators to be trained.

Charlotte taught during the day, but in the evening, Ruth would come to her apartment to talk about the doll's clothes. The two women tossed around concepts for a wardrobe for young women that were tied to their activities, from prom dresses and wedding gowns to athletic wear and office clothing. Because the detail that Ruth demanded required labor-intensive work, Charlotte flew to Japan to arrange for the sewing to be done by workers there.

Charlotte ended up living in Japan for two years, creating twenty-two outfits for Barbie's first wardrobe. Her hotel room at the Imperial Hotel in Tokyo also served as her office.

Charlotte immersed herself in the Japanese garment trade, ordering specialty quality fabrics with small-enough designs to work for the miniature clothes. She checked the fabric thread count to ensure it was as ordered. She would bring a magnifying lens to the fabric factory to inspect material.

Charlotte designed perfect replicas of everything from lingerie to evening gowns. To ensure a perfect fit, she

ABOVE: An original 1958 Lilli doll from Germany, shown here in her tennis outfit. Collectors are willing to pay thousands of dollars for an original in mint condition.

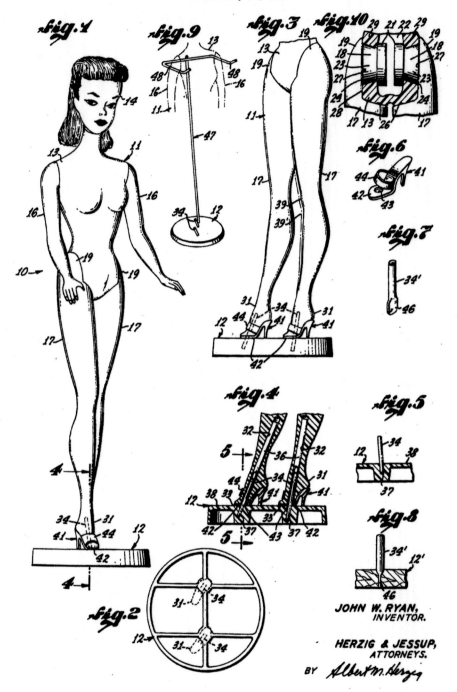

Nov. 21, 1961

J. W. RYAN

3,009,284

DOLL CONSTRUCTION

Filed July 24, 1959

JOHN W. RYAN,
INVENTOR.

HERZIG & JESSUP,
ATTORNEYS.

BY *Albert M. Herzig*

ABOVE: The official U.S. patent for the "Doll Construction" of Barbie was filed on July 24, 1959, by Mattel's designer Jack W. Ryan.

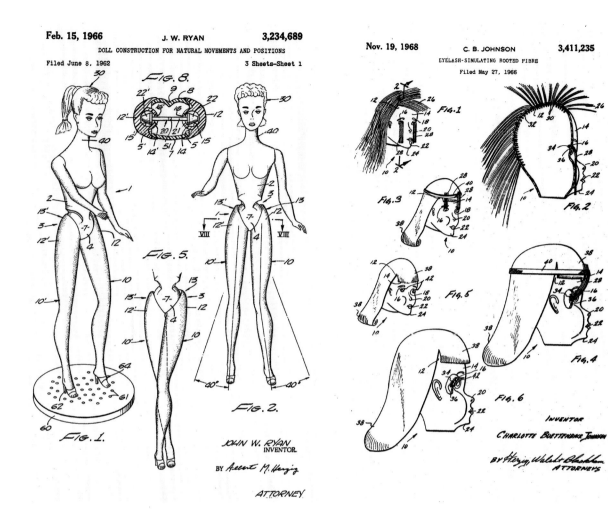

would start with a soft model of the doll, stick pins in it, and then use wax paper and form-fit the doll. In this way, she made patterns that children could easily slide onto the doll's smooth body. Charlotte fought to keep the body uniform so clothes would fit throughout many years and generations of dolls.

She also trained a young Japanese woman named Nakamura Miyatsuka. When Charlotte returned to the United States, Nakamura was left in charge.

Ruth and Charlotte also worked together on the doll's look. Ruth wanted young girls to enjoy brushing the doll's hair, which meant rooting the strands in the head rather than simply gluing them to the scalp. The doll needed shapely lips that were full, but not pouty. The eyes would

be black and white. They glanced slightly to the side and her eyebrows were arched. Her body was impossibly proportioned, but Ruth felt the doll's shape would enhance her clothes. To further show off the fashions in the best way, each of the doll's feet had a hole in the bottom so that she could be placed on a two-pronged posing stand with the name *Barbie!* etched in cursive on its surface.

Ruth had decided that, since her daughter Barbara had inspired her to dream up the doll, it seemed only fitting that the doll bear her name. Once Barbie was named, everything fell into place.

And yet, as the 1959 American Toy Fair in New York City approached, Ruth began to question her choices.

ABOVE: The original U.S. patents filed by designer Jack Ryan for Barbie's "Doll Construction for Natural Movements and Positions," invented by John (Jack) Ryan and filed June 8, 1962 (left), and another for "Eyelash-Simulating Rooted Fibre," invented by Charlotte Johnson and filed on May 27, 1968 (right).

TOP: Ruth Handler and a Mattel sales representative meet with executives from Montgomery Ward, a department store retailer, in Chicago, 1959. BOTTOM: A 1961 Barbie sports a red dress while standing in the living room of her Barbie Dreamhouse. The Dreamhouse, which came with a kitchen, bedroom, and terrace, as well as "built-ins" and "pass-throughs," could be folded away compactly and came with a carrying handle.

The big toys being talked about for Toy Fair that year, as Elliot had predicted, were guns and toy rockets that shot high into the air. If any of the buyers knew about the Barbie doll, they mostly talked about it with the original skepticism that Ruth had encountered at Mattel. They did not believe mothers would buy their daughters a doll with breasts. Even Elliot was still skeptical. Questions entered Ruth's mind:

What if they were right? What if mothers rejected Barbie? Maybe it wasn't enough to put the doll on display and hope people chose her.

Ruth realized that she needed a special approach to marketing, a unique campaign to match her unique doll. She heard about a man she thought could help her, but he was in such high demand that he was difficult to hire.

His name was Ernest Dichter.

ABOVE: Mattel hosts an open house for their City of Industry Facility, circa 1960s. **FOLLOWING**: Mattel's fashion designer, Charlotte Johnson, cuts fabric for a new Barbie design.

chapter 2

BARBIE GOES TO MARKET

Ruth had spent three years creating Barbie when she began to worry. Plans were being made for the American Toy Fair in March of 1959. Ruth envisioned a grand unveiling of the doll, but the skeptics who had grown louder and more numerous as the actual product was slowly revealed. Now the people who needed to support her dream could see the body of the doll, and it was just what everyone had feared. Barbie had grown from an idea into a realistic three-dimensional version of a full-grown woman.

The loud whispers of her doubters made Ruth double down on marketing. Central to her plan was the man Ruth saw as an innovator like herself. He had a worldwide reputation, and provoked both strong praise and strong debate about his methods.

Once again, Ruth was ready to take a risk. She got in touch with Dr. Ernest Dichter and asked him to work for her.

Ernest held a doctorate in psychology from the University of Vienna and was a follower of Freud, but his ambitions took him far beyond any classroom. After fleeing the Nazis in 1938, Ernest landed in New York with a hundred dollars in his pocket and a bold idea for using psychoanalysis to revolutionize consumer marketing.

By the mid-1950s, the majority of Americans had a television in their home, and because it was expensive to own more than one set, they watched together as a family. The picture was black and white and required an antenna to get decent reception, but it was mesmerizing.

The baby boom after World War II led to a flurry of children's programming. There were shows like *Sky King*,

---

OPPOSITE: Mattel's original 1959 Barbie, dressed in her iconic black-and-white swimsuit and holding white sunglasses, complete with metal stand and original packaging.

The Howdy Doody Show, The Roy Rogers Show, Mr. Wizard, Romper Room, and Captain Kangaroo, all airing on only four networks. Under Ruth's guidance, Mattel had been advertising since 1955 on one of the most popular children's shows: The Mickey Mouse Club.

The television ad for the Burp Gun had turned the tables on toy-buying in U.S. households. With ads featuring children—and aimed squarely at their point of view—Mattel had created dedicated consumers. Suddenly, children were begging for toys their parents knew nothing about. This opened the door for more direct toy marketing on shows, including whole cartoons or programs built around particular toys.

While Mattel was going by instinct, Ernest put words to the phenomenon. Touting a psychological focus, he offered his services to companies on the basis that they could sell products by connecting with consumers' unconscious feelings.

He used science to discover why people buy the way they do. This meant understanding the entire person and their self-image.

TOP: Ernest Dichter, American psychologist and marketing expert, was instrumental in working with Mattel's marketing team to ensure Barbie's success in the marketplace.
BOTTOM: Ernest Dichter is shown observing customer shopping behavior during a tour of a supermarket in London on May 6, 1963.

Ernest brought people together. He would ask potential consumers to act like a bowl of pudding or a bar of soap and then describe a product's personality, age, gender, and other characteristics. He took copious notes. The sessions were called "psycho panels." These were the first focus groups.

A big breakthrough came during his work for Betty Crocker. Consumers said they wanted foods that were easy to make at home, but they weren't buying them. Betty Crocker cake mix was the worst seller of this convenience product line.

Ernest brought together a group of wives and mothers to talk about about the cake mix. He realized that they felt guilty about the ease of the mix, even though they liked the convenience. They wanted the activity of baking the cake to be simple, but they also felt that they weren't doing *enough* for their families by only pouring the mix into a bowl and adding water. Ernest realized that the women needed a better sense of participation. He told Betty Crocker executives to rewrite the instructions on the box saying that an egg had to be added, even though the mix didn't need

the egg. Ernest's idea worked. Betty Crocker cake mixes became a huge success.

Ruth was fascinated with marketing and branding. Ernest's focus groups validated Ruth's intuition about the value of role play. She'd seen it in her daughter with the paper dolls, and in other children too, with their Mattel toys.

By the time Ruth contacted him in 1958, Ernest had opened offices around the world and had hundreds of clients.

Ernest signed with Mattel because he was intrigued. He had never worked on a campaign for any toy, and this toy was definitely unusual.

He set out first to find the "story" for Barbie that would get a positive response from consumers and overcome any

ABOVE: Ruth Handler stands next to a display for Barbie Boutique, which hosted examples of various Barbie products, circa 1960.

Once again in 1960, Mattel made an outstanding impression. *Chatty Cathy*, the talking doll, stole the show. "She says eleven different things," was heard whenever two or more toy buyers exchanged information about what toys were "Hot." *Barbie* was spoken of as the most universally "sold out" doll in the country and the byword was to be sure and order enough dolls and costumes for 1960. In just two years, Mattel has become a leading factor in the doll field, accounting for more sales than many old time established doll manufacturers.

In musical toys, our Jacks, Ge-Tars and books are known as the top standards. . . . But this year there was an exciting newcomer, *Strum-Fun Getar*. Here again, buyers labelled the items "Hot."

Next to the government arsenal, ours is the largest in the country. All the guns — from the *Buckle Gun* to the *Winchester* and *Colt 6-Shooter Rifle* were branded as outstanding.

TOY SHOW

Before the Show, hours, days and weeks are spent by the Mattel home office group in pre-planning the "sell" for the year. Because of this pre-planning, we are the only toy company that can give each buyer an advance look at the advertising plan for the year. While the Sales Representative presents the line, he invites the buyer to see all the TV commercials that will be used during the coming year. Buyers are made aware of Mattel's half-hour show, "Matty's Funday Funnies" — which pre-sells 16,000,000 children every week, the year-round.

Each year the Toy Fair "takes over" in New York City during the first week in March. Toy buyers from all over the United States and many foreign countries are invited to see the year's new toy lines. Competition for their attention is keen. The toy industry is unique in that few other industries attract so many ready-to-buy customers to one showcase event. Toy Show is a time for comparison, and to "get the feel" of a new toy. Here the buyers brand a new item as "Hot — A Good Standard — or a Stiff."

With the closing of the Fair, our Sales Representatives return to their individual territories — to begin the important function of holding jobber meetings. This year they are armed with a 30-minute filmed Mattel selling story featuring Clete Roberts, the noted news commentator, in a U.S. News and World Report production of "The Big News for 1960 — Mattel." Out of the planning and work come the orders which fill our production lines. Based on the results of the Toy Show, and the orders received since then, it looks like a very fine year ahead.

ABOVE: A 1960 advertorial demonstrating Mattel's success with many of their toys—including Barbie—at the American Toy Fair in New York City.

Someday

The real world of little girls includes intimate friends like Alice and the Mad Hatter, Dr. Doolittle, Peter and Wendy, Pooh and Piglet, Dorothy and the Tin Woodman, The Little Prince, Beth and Jo and Amy and Meg.

A doll named Barbie© has become a part of this world. With her remarkable wardrobe of meticulously detailed fashions, she represents the glamour and delight of a grown-up world to millions of little girls. Their rich imagination makes Barbie very real, a portrait of themselves when they reach their teens. Barbie is someday.

Your child may see Mattel toys on one of our television programs. If she should ask for that toy, you can be confident of thoughtful originality and uncompromising quality. That quality is important to children . . . and to us. Because ours is a most rewarding business. We make children happy.

© 1961 MATTEL, INC. For a free color print of this photograph (without advertising message), please write to Mattel, Inc., P.O. Box 621, Dept. AD, Hawthorne, California.

ABOVE: Mattel's 1961 "Someday" advertisement featured a brunette Barbie dressed in bridal attire.

hesitation about her body. He understood that the 1950s was a socially conservative time. What story for Barbie would overcome the idea that she represented something outside cultural expectations?

Turning to focus groups, Ernest explored the feelings of children and mothers about Barbie. He wanted them to reveal the personality of Barbie as they saw her. He let them free-associate about the doll, talking about whatever came into their heads. While mothers worried that Barbie was too sexual, girls saw an ideal. They loved her glamour and the possibilities she presented. He was curious that the mothers' mostly negative reactions

softened when they examined the clothes. They were impressed with the quality of the garments and the potential for dressing the doll. And when one mother heard her daughter say, "She is so nicely groomed, Mommy," Ernest heard that to mean that the doll might encourage habits of good hygiene.

A father told Ernest, "When my daughter was a little younger and used to play with dolls, there were many times that I could hear her talking to her doll and repeating word-for-word something her mother might have said to her. If she was feeding the doll, she would use the same words that had been used on her maybe an hour

ABOVE: Barbie's Sew-Free Fashion-Fun by Mattel provided everything junior designers needed to create beautiful doll attire without sewing a stitch, 1963.

earlier. Playing with dolls gives a little girl a chance to be a perfect mimic."

Ernest evaluated these responses and created a plan to bridge the gap between differing views of Barbie: present the doll with a persona as a teenage fashion model. Girls could enjoy the fantasy of a real adult with an enviable job. A fashion model would naturally have a lot of different outfits, and mothers could use the doll to help their daughters learn about looking well-dressed.

Ruth loved Ernest's idea. She had always enjoyed nice clothing and makeup. From the beginning, her vision of Barbie included lipstick, nail polish, and carefully drawn

TOP: Five members of the Official Barbie Fan Club stand next to their collection. **BOTTOM:** Each member of the club received an Official Barbie Fan Club Membership Card like the one shown here.

ABOVE: This 1960s Mattel Family poster showcases members of the Barbie family, including Stacey, Brad, P.J., Casey, Julia, Christie, Tutti, Francie, Skipper, Barbie, and Ken.

ABOVE: Mattel's Wedding Day Barbie, released in 1960, came dressed in a wedding gown and veil, holding a bridal bouquet.

eyebrows. Barbie's original heavy mascara and striking lipstick reflected women's makeup of the day.

Ernest worked closely with the firm creating Ruth's television ads. Together, they gave Ruth what she wanted: an advertising campaign that matched the unique qualities of Barbie.

The first Barbie television commercial was scheduled to air on *The Mickey Mouse Club* in the spring of 1959. It would fully incorporate Ernest's findings.

Filming for the commercial relied on the most sophisticated equipment in the business. Hair stylists stood ready to do touch-ups, as if the doll were a human model. Barbie was posed over and over again while the producers tested her look. The crew faced some unusual challenges, like the dolls' tiny heads melted under the hot, intense lights. The solution? Freeze them overnight, and keep them cold until filming started.

In the commercial, the camera pans over the dolls while soft pop music plays in the background. The melodic, perky voice of a musician sings, "Barbie, you're beautiful. You make me feel my Barbie doll is really real. Barbie's small and so petite. Her clothes and figure look so neat. Her dancing outfit rings the bell. At parties she will cast a spell. Purse and hats and gloves galore, and all the gadgets gals adore."

The first Barbie doll was either blonde or brunette and came dressed in a zebra-striped bathing suit, with black shoes, white sunglasses with blue lenses, and gold hoop earrings. The bathing suit was made with strechable fabric that easily slid in place.

Barbie sold for $3.00, and her outfits ranged from $1.50 upward.

She came in a long, slim cardboard box, fit to her size. In later years, the box would expand to fit sets of Barbie with family and friends, along with clothes and accessories. In 2011, Mattel changed to sustainable packaging, but Barbie's box looked unchanged.

The doll included a small booklet advertising Barbie outfits and accessories. Available sets had names like

ABOVE: A close-up of the original 1959 Barbie. The handpainted heavy black eyeliner and highly arched eyebrows are trademarks of the Number One Barbie (left). Mattel produced tiny book-like catalogues such as this 1961 issue of Barbie and Ken *Teen-Age Fashion Model* (right).

"Cruise Stripes," "Suburban Shopper," "Commuter Set," and "Barbie-Q," which came with kitchen utensils. "Easter Parade" came with a coat, purse, white gloves, pearl necklace and earrings, and shoes. "Picnic Set" included a hat with a tiny plastic frog and flowers on the top, as well as a fishing pole with a sunfish on the hook. In this way, every set became a complete play opportunity as soon as it was opened. Tucked inside there was also a cautionary slip of paper telling girls to "ease leg joints." This was to ensure the legs didn't snap when they were placed onto the small studs that fit into the holes in the bottom of the doll's feet.

Mattel had multiple showrooms at the 1959 American Toy Fair, but Ruth spent most of her time in the room for Barbie. Barbie dolls were arrayed in various outfits and accessories on small stages or stairways that suggested they were in the middle of an activity. Ruth made sure every display was perfect. Every doll adjusted just right in her stand. Each spotlight showed off the dolls to their best advantage.

Of course, there were some glitches in the well-planned rollout of the doll. The manufacturer was late with the boxes to hold Barbie. Luckily, some samples were in the office, although they needed to be glued together by hand.

Attendance was heavy with more than seven thousand people, up from the previous year. Shopping was brisk at the Sheraton-McAlpin and New Yorker hotels, along with the Statler-Hilton and other permanent showrooms in the city. New toys included period dolls from Great Britain with real jewelry, a working soda fountain, a Dr. Seuss zoo, and a plastic infant toy for the high chair or tub.

ABOVE: From left to right, a vintage collection with Barbie Picnic Set (1959) with checked body blouse, clam digger jeans, straw hat, picnic basket, white straw cork-wedge shoes, and fishing gear; Barbie Q ensemble (1959) with rose sundress, white open-toed shoes, chef's hat, and apron that held cooking utensils; and the Resort Set, with red jacket, navy and white striped shirt, white cuffed shorts, white hat, and white vinyl cork-wedge shoes.

Although prices had not gone up from 1958, exhibitors noticed that more high-priced items were on display, and there was a trend toward quality merchandise. In addition, buyers wanted early delivery of toys because retail inventories were low. The stage was set for Mattel.

The buyers showed up to see Barbie. Ruth had anticipated a strong reaction and ordered her Japanese suppliers to double production of dolls and clothes. But the initial enthusiasm of the buyers faded fast as they walked around the room. Three-quarters of the buyers walked out without placing an order, including the powerful buyer from Sears, Roebuck and Co. Just like Elliot and the Mattel research-and-design team had predicted, the toy buyers were skeptical that mothers would allow Barbie into their homes.

By the end of the three days of Toy Fair, Barbie's orders weren't enough to cover production. Ruth was looking at a huge inventory backlog, and worse, the failure of her dream project. She wired Japan to cut production by 40 percent. Elliot found her crying in their hotel room. Ruth felt like a failure.

The months after Toy Fair did not look any better for Barbie's fate. Sales were slow. Inventory backed up. The doll did not seem to be catching on with its intended audience, even though Mattel had taken the unprecedented step of sending retail displays of Barbie dressed in different outfits. Ruth had to cut back orders more, desperate not to end up with a glut of the doll.

But Ruth's tears and fears were premature. Those singable commercials kept playing on television throughout

---

ABOVE: From left to right, a vintage collection with Barbie Suburban Shopper (1959) wearing a blue-and-white sundress, straw hat, and white open-toed heels, carrying a straw purse with fruit; Barbie Roman Holiday (1959) wearing the Cruise Stripes dress, a red-and-white striped coat, red straw hat, short white gloves, black open-toe heels; and Commuter Set Barbie (1959) wearing a navy cardigan suit and jacket, white satin body blouse, a red flower hat, short white gloves, crystal necklace, and navy open-toe heels, and carrying a red hatbox.

NEW! FAMOUS FASHION DOLL CASES— COMPLETE WITH DOLLS!

STANDARD PLASTIC PRODUCTS, INC.
A Subsidiary of Mattel, Inc.

NEW! BARBIE® CASE WITH DOLL #2000

- BARBIE Doll and Beautiful Vinyl Carrying Case Together
- Generous Storage Space for Doll and Clothing

Standard-leg BARBIE is fully visible in see-through window. Full color silk-screened all-around decoration on durable vinyl. 12¼" x 8½" x 2½". Doll in assorted hair colors. Hangers included.
Std. Pack: 6/12 Doz.   Wt: 8 Lbs.

NEW!

SKIPPER® AND SKOOTER® CASE WITH SKIPPER #2001

- SKIPPER Doll and SKIPPER-Sized Vinyl Carrying Case
- Plenty of Storage for Doll and Clothing

Standard-leg SKIPPER is readily visible in clear vinyl window. Brightly decorated all around in silk-screened white polka dots on pink vinyl. 9¾" x 8" x 2½". Doll in assorted hair colors. Hangers included.
Std. Pack: 6/12 Doz.   Wt: 6¼ Lbs.

NEW! SKIPPER® AND SKOOTER® CASE WITH SKOOTER #2002

Same as above, except with standard-leg SKOOTER doll in assorted hair colors.

ABOVE: Mattel's 1966 advertisement for fashion doll cases—one for Barbie, and another for additions to the Barbie line, Skipper and Skooter—both of which come with a doll, and have space for storage, including hangers.

the spring, and even though *The Mickey Mouse Club* was showing reruns in its final season, children were watching. When school let out, Barbie dolls started flying out of stores. Supply couldn't keep up with demand. Girls wanted more than one Barbie, which meant they needed even more clothes. It took Mattel three years to catch up with the backlog of orders.

Opening a Barbie box was magical. After years of holding pudgy baby dolls, or fragile display dolls—some made of porcelain with delicate clothing—Barbie was sturdy. She could be held in one hand, even by a young girl. Her clothes were easy to get on and off, and play value came not only from imagining Barbie as a real woman

TOP: A hostess checks the Barbie exhibition at a toy fair in Paris, France, February 4, 1967. **BOTTOM**: Skipper and Skooter trifold doll case from 1965, showing the interior of the case with Skooter and accessories.

washington square

WELCOME HOME DEBBIE
HALF MILLIONTH MEMBER
BARBIE FAN CLUB
TODAY AT 4

Welcome Home
DEBBIE
Half-Millionth
Member
BARBIE FAN CLUB

performing various activities, but also looking at her clothing catalog.

The first true "fashion doll" had been born. Girls no longer saw dolls as their babies, but as themselves. The doubters had asked, "How do you give a child a woman's body to play with?" Ruth had shown that Mattel trusted children and she had been right.

By the end of that year, 351,000 dolls had been sold. A global icon was born. Ruth was thrilled when she would get on an airplane, or be out shopping, and see a child holding a Barbie.

Ruth figured Barbie would sell for about three years, and then interest would peter out like for most toys. But Ruth's creation exceeded her wildest dreams. By 1965, Barbie had a fan club of more than six hundred thousand members, second only to the membership of Girl Scouts of the United States of America. Hundreds of thousands more joined clubs in Europe. By 1968, Ruth was a "lady millionaire," a "Woman of the Year," and the well-known "mother" of Barbie.

Barbie fueled huge growth for Mattel. By 1970, Barbie and related products had brought in more than $600 million in

ABOVE: A young girl named Debbie was the 500,000th member of the Official Barbie Fan Club.

ABOVE: Tracy Blanchette became Mattel's sweepstakes contest winner by being the one-millionth member of the Official Barbie Fan Club in 1965.

revenue. Mattel was a global operation. Ruth had offices in Canada, Central and South America, Western Europe, Asia, and Australia. There were more than five million square feet of office, research, manufacturing, and warehouse space, and twenty thousand workers.

Barbie also became a sought-after collectible, along with all the subsequently released friends, family, clothing, and accessories. She created hundreds of thousands of passionate followers worldwide.

In 2018, at the National Barbie Doll Collector Convention, Bradley Justice received a unique honor. Bradley was named "Barbie's Best Friend" for his work with *Doll News Magazine* and his research and preservation of the Barbie collection at the United Federation of Doll Clubs.

For Bradley, his love of Barbie started at five years old with a popular version of the doll created that year. "I first met Barbie in 1975," Bradley explained. "I spent the summer with my mom's side of the family in the eastern part of North Carolina, and my cousin Caroline had just gotten Sweet 16 Barbie. She had a trunk full of Barbie and Ken, and we played together with the dolls. I was smitten with Sweet 16, thought she was the most gorgeous thing I'd ever seen."

He saved his five-dollar-per-week allowance to buy Barbie dolls, along with clothing and accessories. His two brothers had other dolls popular at the time, like G.I. Joe and *Star Trek* characters. Bradley would spend hours making up stories that involved all the dolls. Bradley said, "I always had this crazy imagination and would get frustrated with friends who didn't know how to play make-believe. That's what kids grasped from the first Barbie commercial—that Barbie was for playing make-believe, and they ran with it."

But at eleven years old, Bradley saw a program on television with Sybil DeWein, who wrote a book about Barbie collecting, *The Collectors Encyclopedia of Barbie Dolls and Collectibles*. DeWein talked about how the first Barbie was worth hundreds of dollars.

After that, Bradley spent his weekends at garage sales or flea markets looking for Barbie or her clothes and accessories at a discount. He would buy an item for five dollars that would be worth hundreds of times that amount. This was a fun and lucrative "job" for a teenager.

ABOVE: The original 1959 Number One Barbie, with black-and-white zebra-striped strapless swimsuit and black open-toe heels, is one of the most sought-after dolls in the Barbie collection.

Throughout his teenage years, Bradley pursued his collecting passion. By the time college came along, Bradley had enough duplicates and triplicates to pay for food, books, and other expenses. He graduated with a degree in merchandising and marketing.

Bradley explained that selecting Barbies in the early days meant navigating an underground network. A lot of dealers did not acknowledge that Barbie was collectible, but later, "the list" was created. In those pre-Internet days, you would send a dealer a self-addressed stamped envelope with a list of what you had and what you wanted. It took Bradley five years to find the Golden Glamour outfit from 1965, with its very detailed, complicated items, including a fur hat, long gloves, and spiked shoes.

Bradley found a Number Three Barbie at a thrift store for a dollar. It was in pristine condition, with great skin tone and perfect hair—the kind of find that makes a collector very happy. Over the years, Bradley realized that he was a "catch-and-release" collector, meaning he would find dolls, but was also willing to sell them.

What is so fascinating about the first editions of Barbie? Bradley explained that they represent "fashion in miniature." Everything about them was new. "With Barbie, nothing had existed before, everything had to be created for her. People were fascinated with her being miniature and tiny, but also with the glamour and detail. You wanted everything about Barbie, which was why she was destined to create a collector culture."

Bradley was also the Region 8 director for the United Federation of Doll Clubs and curator for the Doll and Miniature Museum of High Point, North Carolina. He continues to be a tireless researcher of Barbie history, with special focus on Charlotte Johnson, Barbie's first clothing designer.

To sum up his relationship with Barbie, Bradley said, "She's monumental, cultural, iconic, and generations have played with her, including grandmothers, mothers, daughters, and sons. Each generation approaches Barbie a little bit differently, and each play pattern is a little different, because children's lives change with the times. But Barbie will always be there with them."

ABOVE: Barbie is shown wearing the yellow Sweet Dreams outfit from 1959. **FOLLOWING:** The millionth Barbie doll arrives in Germany, 1965.

chapter 3

BREAKING
BOUNDARIES

Barbie started out as a teenage fashion model, but she has come a long way from that first job, and she still has a long way to go. Barbie "careers" have reflected not only the broad range of women's roles in the world, but also their aspirations. She has gone beyond early expectations of how children would play with her.

In 1963, *The Saturday Evening Post* wrote, "Mattel has proved that girls in the nine to thirteen age group want a doll not to mother but as a means of looking ahead to the days of the pizza party, the football weekend, and the Junior Prom."

This view of girls' dreams and imaginations proved to be too narrow.

In the 1960s, girls wrote to Mattel with questions like, "Why doesn't Barbie have a parachuting outfit?" Ruth read the comments, and Mattel responded. The runway may have been where Barbie took her first steps, but by 1965 she had been a fashion editor, singer, executive ("career girl"), and student teacher.

Barbie became an astronaut before the first American woman, Sally Ride, went into space. Astronaut Barbie also went to the pretend moon four years before American Neil Armstrong took his amazing walk and said the famous words, "That's one small step for a man, one giant leap for mankind."

Barbie won an Olympic gold medal not long after the 1972 Olympics in Munich. She also had the courage to become a surgeon at a time when the total number of women physicians in the United States was around 5 percent.

OPPOSITE: A young French girl poses in 1965 with her new Christmas toys: Miss Astronaut Barbie and Mr. Astronaut Ken, ready for their journey in space.

In the 1980s, women were training to become veterinarians, so Barbie took up that profession. And thanks to the growing popularity of music videos, Barbie dolls became rock stars.

The 1990s were a breakout decade for Barbie. In 1992, Americans elected more women to Congress than ever before. It was the "Year of the Woman" and Barbie kept up with modern culture by entering a number of careers that had traditionally been reserved for men.

Barbie was a Marine Corps sergeant, a business executive, and most notably, a candidate for President of the United States. At the time, there had never been a

woman candidate from a major party on the presidential ballot. Barbie was chasing the dream.

In 1993, Barbie became an army medic and a police officer. Two years later, she was a firefighter in a bright yellow uniform, although less than 2 percent of firefighters in the United States were women at that time. Before the decade closed, Barbie entered two more nontraditional jobs, becoming a dentist and a commercial airline pilot. She also hit a home run as a Major League Baseball player in 1998. Barbie has always been ahead of her time!

In 2004, Barbie again ran for president, this time in a television-ready, apple-red pantsuit. The 2000s saw

ABOVE: From left to right, a collection showing some of Barbie's many careers, such as Astronaut Barbie (1965) wearing a silver spacesuit, white helmet, and brown boots; Surgeon Barbie (1973) wearing light blue scrubs, a face mask, cap, and stethoscope, and holding a towel; and Rockstar Barbie (1986) wearing a hot pink jacket with matching leggings, a pink and silver dress, and white boots, holding a white microphone.

Barbie caring for babies as a neonatal doctor, dancing as a ballerina, and coaching her soccer team.

Again and again, Barbie's broken new ground as an architect, a race car driver, or a computer engineer. And in a third election campaign, Barbie ran for president in 2012, wearing a signature pink jacket with matching skirt.

Of course, from the very beginning, girls understood that Barbie could be anything they imagined, and also, reflect back the emotional journey they themeselves, experienced.

In one of those early focus groups, an eight-year-old said, "I could pretend she was going out to dinner, or going on a trip for the summer and afterwards going to college, and the years pass and she gets married. I could pretend she was going to the library to get out books, and I was the librarian showing her around."

This girl went on to explain what must have been a traumatic experience for her or someone she knew, showing Barbie's potential from the beginning to help children deal with their emotional life. "She could be going on a honeymoon. Her husband has a big boat . . . They go to the country, play ball . . . They went swimming . . . She got pregnant. She got sick and after the baby was due, in a week, the baby died. They had to take the baby away."

ABOVE: From left to right, a collection of Barbie's careers continues with Army Medic Barbie (1993) wearing full camouflage, and a red beret, and holding two green army bags; President Barbie (2004) dressed in a red pantsuit, and a scarf, and carrying a black bag; and Architect Barbie (2011) wearing a blue ombre dress with hot pink trim, a black jacket, black boots, glasses, and white hard hat, and holding a document-carrying tube for blueprints.

thank you for
Raising your
voice! ♥ The Barbie
Team

ABOVE: The Zendaya Barbie (2015), created in the likeness of Zendaya Coleman—a singer, actress, dancer, and model. Michelle Chidoni, a spokesperson for Mattel at the time, said of Zendaya, "She's a role model who is focused on standing up for yourself, your culture, and for what you believe in—that's very relevant for girls."

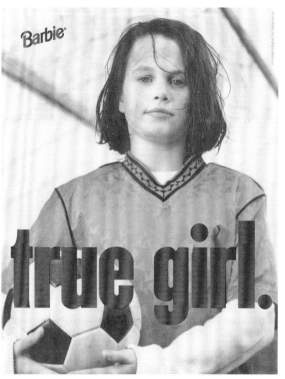

ABOVE: A collection of posters from Mattel's 1999 Barbie campaign.

This research into how children reacted to Barbie has informed the brand's evolution over the decades. Today's massive surveys help Mattel understand what consumers prefer, and their thinking about a new toy. For instance, the Barbie line of inspirational dolls involved asking 80,000 mothers worldwide about what they would like to see in a doll, and what their concerns were for their daughters.

A whopping 86 percent worried about the role models that their daughters saw around them.

Responding to that need, in 2015, Barbie designers came up with an exceptional group of Shero Barbie dolls, which included famed director Ava DuVernay, who directed many important projects such as *Selma*, *13th*, and *When They See Us*, and Olympic fencer Ibtihaj Muhammad. In 2018, Mattel expanded the Shero group with "Inspirational Women," a fascinating group of Barbie dolls—such as the actress, singer, and dancer Zendaya Coleman—that arrived in time for International Women's Day on March 8. The new Barbie dolls represented the largest lineup of role models in the doll's history. As Mattel put it, "You can't be what you can't see."

What makes a Shero, or an inspirational woman? There are many answers to that question, but the women chosen to be portrayed as Barbie dolls share a positive attitude, passion for their jobs, courage, and an interest in helping other people. They are women who respect others, who are willing to speak up, take risks, and are generous leaders.

Here are some of the Inspirational Women and how their dolls were accessorized:

Patty Jenkins is a dynamic, award-winning film director, best known for the blockbuster hit *Wonder Woman*, which was the highest-grossing film of the summer and the third-highest of the year in 2017. Mattel modeled a Barbie doll after her, complete with a camera.

Chloe Kim is an American snowboarding champion. In the 2018 Winter Olympics, she became the youngest woman to win a medal in the women's snowboard halfpipe. The Barbie doll in her image came dressed in a yellow jacket and camouflage snowgear, and equipped a white snowboard.

Get inspired to protect the environment with Bindi Irwin, a committed conservationist who is also a star on

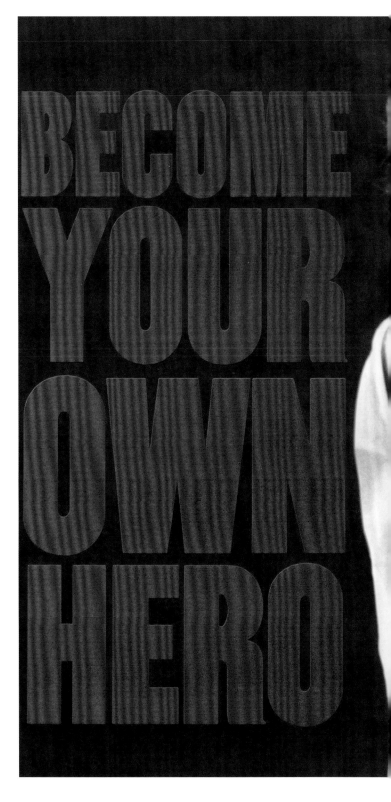

ABOVE: "Become Your Own Hero" poster from Mattel's 1999 Barbie campaign designed to inspire and empower girls.

Australian television and a champion on *Dancing with the Stars*. Mattel created a Bindi Irwin doll dressed in khakis and accompanied by a friendly koala.

Go for the knockout with Nicola Adams, a British boxing champion in the flyweight division. After winning two gold medals, she was awarded an Order of the British Empire (OBE), the second highest honor her country can give. Nicola's doll wore a black-and-white training jacket.

Ride the wind with Çağla Kubat, a champion windsurfer and sailor from Turkey. She has a degree in mechanical engineering and has also been a model and an actress. The doll came dressed in a pink and blue wet suit, ready to take on the waves.

Get cooking with Hélène Darroze, a French chef, who has earned coveted Michelin stars for her restaurants. She's a fourth-generation chef who loves to bring people pleasure through food. She's also a knight, admitted to the French Legion of Honor in 2012. Her doll was dressed in a stylish crisp, white, double-breasted chef's coat.

Spike the ball with Hui Ruoqi, a volleyball champion from China. She started playing in elementary school and was part of the team that won Olympic Gold in 2016. She has a shelf full of medals: a silver medal from the 2014 World Championships, a bronze medal from the 2011 Japan World Cup, and two gold medals from the Asian Championship. Sporting a perky ponytail, her doll was dressed in a white tank top and red shorts, and she carried a yellow and blue soccer ball as an accessory.

Knitting her way to the top is Leyla Piedayesh, an Iranian-born German fashion designer and entrepreneur. She was first inspired by a pair of knitted wrist warmers that she found at a flea market. She began knitting her own creations. Leyla now owns the wildly popular fashion label Lala Berlin.

Hit the long drive with Lorena Ochoa, a professional golfer who caught the world's attention. At eleven years old, she knew she wanted to be the best. She achieved her goal, as well as a place in the World Golf Hall of Fame. She was the top-ranked female golfer for 158 consecutive weeks and the first Mexican golfer to be ranked number one in the world.

Travel with Martyna Wojciechowska, Editor in Chief of *National Geographic Poland*. Known for writing about her

ABOVE: A Shero Barbie in the likeness of boxing champion Nicola Adams, wearing black and white shorts and training jacket with gold trim, white high tops, and white boxing gloves (2018).

adventures, she's climbed the highest mountains on all seven continents. Her doll was dressed in smart black pants and top, accented with a pale green jacket.

Go for the goal with Sara Gama, a soccer player from Italy. She was the team captain in the 2008 European Championship.

A star of the big screen, Xiaotong Guan was born into an acting family and has been a star in movies and television in her native China since she was a child. She is known for her roles in the films *Nuan*, *The Promise*, and *The Left Ear*, and the television series *To Be a Better Man*. In 2017, she became the ambassador for "World Life Day," a joint campaign by the United Nations Environment Programme, International Fund for Animal Welfare, and The Nature Conservancy.

Looking to the heroes of the past, Amelia Earhart was the first woman to fly solo across the Atlantic Ocean. In 1923, she received the sixteenth international pilot's license ever issued to a woman, and went on to set many flying records and write best-selling books. She even started a line of pilot-inspired clothes that was advertised in *Vogue* magazine. Her doll was dressed in a brown bomber jacket, bodysuit, scarf, goggles, and a helmet—ready for takeoff!

Paint the world with Frida Kahlo, a Mexican artist who created haunting self-portraits and vivid, imaginative flowers, influencing an entire generation of artists. She described herself as a child who went around "in a world of colors." She loved to look dramatic, wearing arresting colors and putting bright flowers in her black hair. Her doll came dressed in a long traditional Mexican dress, a fringed red shawl, and a floral headpiece.

Number the stars with Katherine Johnson, a NASA mathematician, physicist, and one of the first African-American women to work on the complex mathematical equations that led to space flight. She started high school at ten years old, going on to be one of the great mathematicians of her day. When NASA switched to computers, they had Katherine double-check the accuracy of the results. Katherine's story drove the #1 New York Times bestseller and subsequent hit movie *Hidden Figures*. Her doll wore a collared pink dress with pleats, stylish glasses, and a NASA name badge.

ABOVE: The Gabby Douglas Barbie doll, released in 2018, celebrates the accomplishments of this extraordinary gymnast and role model, dressed in a pink and black Nike tracksuit over a stars-and-stripes leotard.

ABOVE: Three dolls from the 2017 Barbie Inspiring Women series pay tribute to the incredible heroines of their time, including (from left to right) aviation hero Amelia Earhart, artist Frida Kahlo, and NASA mathematician Katherine Johnson.

Ibtihaj Muhammad is an American sabre fencer and a member of the United States fencing team. In 2016, she won a bronze medal in the Rio de Janeiro games, becoming the first female Muslim American athlete to earn an Olympic medal. Her doll wore in a white fencing outfit, including her hijab and her fencing mask, accessorized by a silver-handled fencing sabre.

Ashley Graham, an American model and body activist, is hailed for breaking stereotypes and is known for her accessibility and body confidence. She celebrates what real women's bodies look like rather than standards set by the media and fashion industry and has been described as an "ambassador of the real beauty movement." Her curvy doll was dressed wearing a sparkly black dress with a denim jacket.

Misty Copeland, an acclaimed prima ballerina, was considered a child prodigy who quickly rose among the ranks and became the first African-American to be appointed to principal dancer. She loves giving back and has worked with many charitable organizations dedicated to mentoring young people. In 2015, she was named one of *Time* magazine's "100 Most Influential People." Her doll was dressed in a striking red bodysuit and tutu, with matching toulle hairpiece.

American film director, writer, and producer Ava DuVernay became the first African American female director to receive nominations for both a Golden Globe and an Academy Award for Best Picture. In 2016, she directed an Oscar-nominated documentary about the criminalization of African Amercians and the U.S. prison system. Her doll had long, braided hair, and was wearing a sleek black outfit, charm bracelet, and white heels.

Mental health activist and model Adwoa Aboah was thrilled to be recognized by Mattel. On her public Instagram account, Aboah wrote, "My very own Barbie! It's mad! Seeing my own doll that has my skin color, shaved head, freckles, and my tattoos is beyond mad. I spent the majority of my childhood wishing for blonde hair, pining over Barbie's light skin and blue eyes. All those years ago and I didn't feel like I was represented anywhere. But today with my big toothy grin, I feel so very proud to have been

ABOVE: Model and activist Adwoa Aboah poses with her Shero Barbie doll, released March 6, 2019.

awarded this Shero doll for all the hard work I have put into myself and @gurlstalk. All I hope is that some little girl out there sees this and realizes that her wildest dreams are possible if she puts her mind to it. I hear you and see you, this doll is for you."

Ruth Handler died in 2002. Her life and legacy were the inspiration behind the first Entrepreneur Barbie, introduced in 2014. For this line of dolls, Mattel collaborated with female-founded and -led companies like Girls Who Code, Rent the Runway, and Plum Alley.

Reshma Saujani started and runs the nonprofit Girls Who Code. The group works to support and increase the number of women in computer science. Key to their mission is changing the image of what a computer programmer looks like.

Saujani works with lots of young girls who play with dolls. And girls need role models to think about who they want to be. She remembers a Barbie when she was young that looked like she was from India. Having Barbie dolls of different races lets girls see themselves reflected. Saujani hopes women will take risks, do something hard, and not be discouraged by others telling them they can't do what they want to do, including coding.

ABOVE: (From left to right) The Barbie Look: Lace Dress Doll, Barbie Careers Cupcake Chef, Totally Hair 25th Anniversary Barbie Doll, and the Barbie Ice Skater Doll are just some of the popular dolls that inspire girls to dream big!

At Plum Alley, women entrepreneurs can get funding to start a business through a crowd-funded source. Deborah Jackson, one of the founders, is passionate about women stepping up, owning companies, raising money, becoming successful, and generating their own wealth. She says the Entrepreneur Barbie doll can help not only girls, but also fathers and boys, to see the capabilities of female entreprenuers. She loves that Barbie has a broad range of careers, just like the women she funds who have limitless ideas.

Rent the Runway is the place to go online for women to rent designer dresses and accessories. Jennifer Fleiss is a cofounder of the company. She wants women of all ages to dream bigger and believes that Barbie encourages them to do that from the time they are little girls.

Ruth Handler would be pleased to hear the words of these modern women who recognize the essential and enduring value of Barbie. What Ruth envisioned still represents vision and opportunity to millions of women and girls worldwide.

TOP: Academy Award–winning director Ava DuVernay poses with the Barbie doll made in her likeness in 2015. **BOTTOM**: Ballerina Misty Copeland poses with the doll made in her likeness, complete with vibrant bodysuit and headpiece in 2016.

chapter 4

SHAPING BARBIE

Humans have made dolls for thousands of years. Early dolls in Egypt and Greece were made of wood or clay and were used in religious ceremonies.

In other lands, cloth and animal bone, corn husks, and bark, all served to make human representations and grew to be part of children's imaginative play.

Over time, dolls became more sophisticated and elaborate. Artisans in Germany and France made exquisite dolls from porcelain. In America, children cherished dolls from the Old World and also played with new ones from wood and clay.

When Ruth Handler first conceived of the Barbie doll, she knew that the detail she wanted could only be made from polystyrene. This type of plastic was the main raw material for the special injection-molding process that Ruth envisioned.

When Frank Nakamura went to Japan to work on Mattel's doll house furniture, he was also tasked with finding a factory that could make the dolls that Ruth wanted. It wasn't easy.

The first polystyrene plant had just been completed near Nagoya in 1957. Japan was ready to "bake" plastic bowls, cups, glasses, food containers, electrical appliances, and toys, but no one had "baked" a Barbie doll before. Everything was an experiment.

At the plant, metal molds were made for Barbie's head, legs, arms, and body. Each mold had multiple cavities so that more than one part could be made at once. The cavities were filled with a liquid mixture and then closed tight.

As the mold heated up and turned, the material was pulled by centrifugal force into every crevice. After the heat was turned off inside the oven, the molds were slowly cooled by air and cold water. The finished pieces were taken out. If needed, trimming was done by hand for any excess plastic.

OPPOSITE: Designers carefully paint lips and eyes on the dolls by hand.

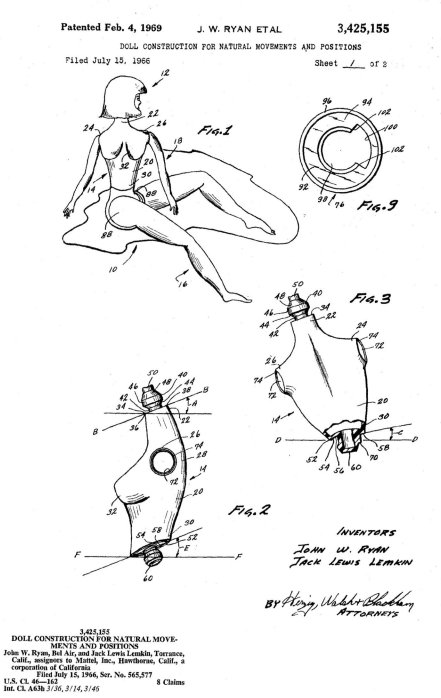

United States Patent Office

3,425,155
Patented Feb. 4, 1969

Patented Feb. 4, 1969   J. W. RYAN ET AL   3,425,155

DOLL CONSTRUCTION FOR NATURAL MOVEMENTS AND POSITIONS

Filed July 15, 1966   Sheet _1_ of 2

INVENTORS
JOHN W. RYAN
JACK LEWIS LEMKIN

BY Herzig, Walsh & Blackburn
ATTORNEYS

3,425,155
**DOLL CONSTRUCTION FOR NATURAL MOVE-
MENTS AND POSITIONS**
John W. Ryan, Bel Air, and Jack Lewis Lemkin, Torrance,
Calif., assignors to Mattel, Inc., Hawthorne, Calif., a
corporation of California
Filed July 15, 1966, Ser. No. 565,577
U.S. Cl. 46—162   8 Claims
Int. Cl. A63h 3/36, 3/14, 3/46

ABOVE: Mattel's U.S. Patent for "Doll Construction for Natural Movements and Positions," filed by designer Jack Ryan on June 15, 1966.

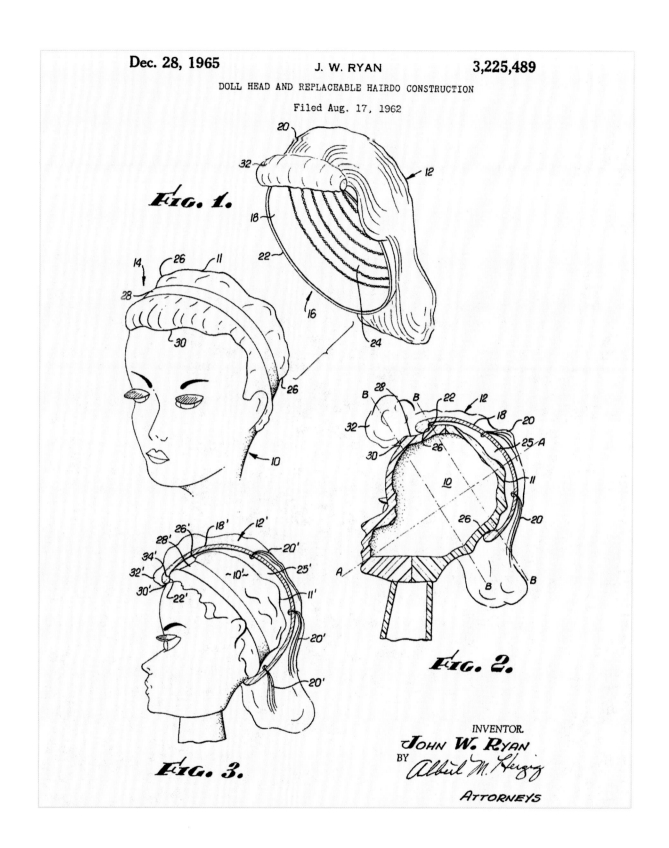

Those first Barbies couldn't be assembled until her face was painted by hand, using tiny brushes. In later years, a head-sized mask, like a stencil, was created that exposed places on Barbie's face that could be spray-painted. This created more uniform makeup.

Barbie's bald head was covered with nylon hair rooted in the vinyl. Special sewing machines, operated by hand, put the hair in place. A comb-out came next, and finally a trim, and then, Barbie was ready to have her head attached.

After Barbie's bathing suit was slipped on, she was placed into her narrow box and finally shipped across the ocean to stores.

Over time, Barbie production moved from Japan to Indonesia and Chang'an, China. Despite these developments, the way Barbie was made fundamentally did not change. What changed, however, was the marketing, and the way women and girls related to their dolls.

Isela Scaglione, Vice President Portfolio Management at Mattel, explained, "Millennial audiences wanted something more meaningful and purposeful, and made us rethink how we were marketing the brand. We look back to the past to guide the future, and that's how we're most successful, and right now being a purposeful brand is important.

ABOVE: A collection of vintage career dolls. From left to right, the Busy Gal Fashion Barbie (1960), Registered Nurse Barbie (1961), American Airlines Stewardess (1961), and Career Girl Barbie Doll (1963).

"Storytelling has shifted from the things Barbie has, to what she does. In the past, there was a focus on a boyfriend or shoes, but now relationships have greater importance, along with the idea of being anything. What does Barbie enable in a girl?"

From that foundation, designers brought their creativity and imagination to the process. What dolls, clothes, and accessories match the cultural moment and the brand's narrative for Barbie?

Robert Best, Vice President of Barbie Product Design, said, "You're always looking at culture through sites like Pinterest, or bloggers, or fashion websites and fashion apps. Just like in the old days, there are also still magazines and books. But inspiration can come from going to a museum exhibit like the *Heavenly Bodies* exhibit at the Metropolitan Museum of Art in New York City." Designers take their ideas and build a "mood board," which shows what cultural references are informing their design. Best said, "How do you communicate the idea of culture, what's cool, what's hip, what makes a celebrity the one that's wildly popular? It's like catching lightning in a bottle."

From the beginning to today, Barbie is, at her core, a business. Every product in the brand also uses an analysis of costs and timing required for big stores like Walmart and Target. Companies that sell the Barbie brand have different requirements and different dates for when they need products. All these decisions require precise planning. There are two main seasons in the toy cycle. For the spring season, toys must be shipped right after Christmas. For the Christmas season, toys must be shipped by the first of June.

These deadlines drive the process, and there are many meetings between departments in the Barbie brand to approve the steps that get a product from idea to market.

ABOVE: From left to right, sketches that inspired the fashions for Barbie: Red Flare (1962), After Five (1962), Dinner at Eight (1963), and Orange Blossom (1961).

As Scaglione explained, "Once we know the design and review samples, we have to build the tools and tool design, then we cut the tools out of blocks of steel and debug them to make sure that the mold is perfect. When we take out the final plastic piece, we want it to be perfect."

Robert Best added, "We have development partners overseas who are our liaisons on the ground with the factory, and they can use a sketch that we send them as a road map, so that's a jumping-off point for them. If you look at a Fashionista doll, the plant can produce a prototype from a general outline. They know the body is going to be one of several. If it's soft goods, meaning fabric, it has to be sewn, and the digital programs can't replicate fabric, so you have to see the real thing. That's why they have to ship a prototype to us, which can take a few days."

Doll design involves everything from head to toe, just like fashion. All aspects are in the designers' purview, from clothing, to hair and makeup, to how the face is sculpted.

The team must also look at the ability to reuse items. They want to minimize waste. Every change has broad implications. For instance, a flat-footed Barbie was introduced because women don't always wear high heels. That meant none of Barbie's old shoes would fit the new doll. As Best said, "Manufacturing excels in simplicity, because it's more efficient. Variety is the enemy of manufacturing because it's less efficient."

ABOVE: A few of the various stages in creating new Barbie doll models, including (from top to bottom) sculpting the head out of clay, creating metal casts for molds, and applying hair and makeup before assembly.

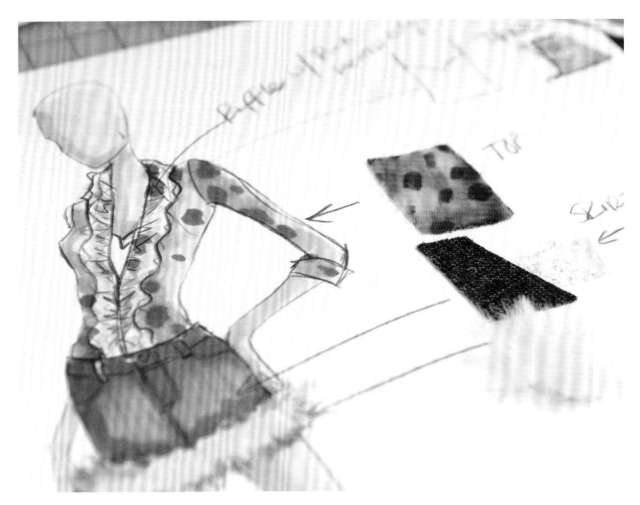

The brand team is always looking at making exciting new offerings and attracting new fans, even as they consider the complicated process of bringing items to market.

Things occasionally go wrong. There may be issues with the art on the box, with a fabric's feel, or with parts that don't fit quite right. There may be a need for color adjustment or other tweaks.

The 2018 Yves Saint Laurent (YSL) dolls are an example of commitments made with outside partners and how the Barbie team worked to fulfill them. Mattel reached out to YSL executives to see if they would be interested in allowing their dresses to be recreated for Barbie. Scaglione explained, "Barbie is a big influence for designers, as well as a product that is influenced by them. We look for partnerships that inspire us, or that we can inspire. So, because of Yves Saint

Laurent's standing in the high-fashion industry, we felt it would be a win-win to bring that high fashion to a different set of people."

No YSL design had ever been licensed outside the brand before. But YSL agreed, and three dolls, sculpted in the images of the models who first wore the designs, were created to wear the iconic fashions. Only a thousand pieces of each garment were made. Commitments were made by Mattel at every step of the design, including quality, color, and authenticity, right down to how the dresses were constructed. The famous Mondrian dress had each of its geometric solid color patches sewn together separately, same as on the original YSL dresses.

Fashion is a form of self-expression and culture, and Barbie parallels that, even down to her face paint. A good

ABOVE: A rough designer's sketch with mood board, complete with fabric samples. This design would become part of the 2005 Fashion Fever Barbie Animal Print Collection.

ABOVE: A set of Yves Saint Laurent dolls honoring the French fashion designer, which are part of a limited platinum collection of Barbie dolls, released in 2018. There were fewer than one thousand made of each doll.

example is Malibu Barbie, where the doll looks straight ahead, rather than to the side. Another example, Barbie's initial heavily outlined eyes, blue shadow, and red lips were the palette for 1950s women, but when lips turned pale, so did Barbie's.

At the American Toy Fair in 1959, Ruth was not satisfied with the face of the first Barbie, which was molded by a Japanese sculptor named Kohei Suzuki. It wasn't until Barbie Number Three, released in 1960, that Ruth felt that the arched eyebrows had been smoothed enough to soften her look. Her heavy black eyeliner disappeared as well, giving her a younger appearance.

According to Hiroe Okubo-Worf, one of the early painters, there was a face design competition to figure out which painters could do the best job. Okubo-Worf's talent stood out, and for many years she was the sole face painter for Barbie. She saw many changes, including 1967's Twist 'n Turn with deep red lips, rosy cheekbones, and large blue eyes with long lashes. Malibu Barbie recieved a smile showing her teeth in 1971. In 1979, Kissing Barbie

---

ABOVE: Two Gold Label Barbie dolls for the adult collector, including the Versace Barbie doll, released in 2004 (left), and the Oscar de la Renta Barbie doll, released in 2016 (right).

was sold with a pucker that could be relaxed through a button on the back. The introduction of the International Dolls series in 1980 meant further changes in face sculpting and painting.

Barbies have been designed to look like actual people, including celebrities and notables from the Shero and Inspiring Women lines. These dolls mirror the looks of the extraordinary women they are celebrating through face shape, paint, hair, and body. Equally challenging for the artists are the Fashionista dolls because each Barbie has a unique face. There are more than forty Fashionista dolls, with more being created all the time by Mattel artists. Once a sculpt is approved, it goes to the plant, where they create a rapid prototype using three-dimensional printing, a process almost unimaginable in the 1950s. From there, designers can make changes and move to the approvals that will get Barbie to market.

Perhaps the most dramatic sculpting change for Barbie came in 2016 when her single iconic body type was expanded. Kimberly Culmone, Senior Vice President, Head of Design Dolls at Mattel, Inc., told the inside story of Barbie's new bodies.

Kim was the first in her family to go to college. She earned a degree in interior design and then a second degree in fabric design. When she decided to build her resume with an in-house job, she found a temporary assignment at Mattel in Textile Engineering. That was the department that developed fabrics for all Mattel toys, including Barbie.

"All of a sudden," Kim recalled, "my mind was blown. I hadn't really thought about the idea that someone had to design Barbie! There were all these fantastic artists that were doing painting, textiles, hair, fashion. I realized I could take my love as a kid and my textile background and put them together." Soon after Kim took on her new position, Barbie sales slowed. Everyone agreed that a revolution was needed, and top leadership was saying they were open to ideas they hadn't been open to before.

Changing Barbie's body had been a topic for a long time. It was obvious from the marketplace that there was

ABOVE: The Kissing Barbie doll, released in 1979, was dressed in a sheer pale-pink nylon dress with a floral and kiss imprint pattern with a tiny pink nylon ribbon accent, and pink superstar shoes. The Kissing Barbie came with a bouquet of pink and purple plastic flowers, and play lipstick for Barbie.

ABOVE: Mattel released a series of Dolls of the World in the Barbie Signature Line. Shown from left to right are the first Hispanic Barbie, released in 1979, and the first Black Barbie, released in 1968.

ABOVE: In 1997, Mattel announced a special edition Barbie friend named "Share-a-Smile Becky," who used a pink and purple wheelchair, and came with two friendship necklaces.

a desire to explore new body types. But the idea hadn't always tested well in terms of consumer demand.

Kim said, "I went to my family of designers and asked, 'What have you always wanted to do that you've never done before? If you were Ruth Handler today, how would you want to live up to our promise of being reflective of the times, and being inspiring of limitless potential for children?'" Her team bet on changes that reflected diversity and inclusion, and the bet paid off.

Barbie's traditional blue eyes and blonde hair grew to a more inclusive reflection of society. Barbie's perpetual high heel also became a flexible version that could be a flat or high heel-shaped foot, as well as a permanently flat version. While Barbie had long reflected other ethnicities through skin tone, the team began to change the sculpts for her face to reflect ethnic characteristics. And, perhaps most dramatically, Barbie's famous figure became just one of four body types: original, curvy, petite, and tall.

Diversity and inclusion rose to the top of concerns for designers and marketing. And once they opened the door to Barbie's presentation, they suddenly saw things they had not seen before, like the way Barbie looked in illustrations and on media platforms. Kim said, "The culture is also showing more diversity and inclusion, and we're watching and being responsive."

The best-selling doll in 2017 was a curvy Fashionista. Kim's department is committed to thinking of ways to support the values of diversity and inclusion held by the brand. A line of differently abled dolls, one in a wheelchair and one with a prosthetic leg, were introduced in 2019. Kim explained, "We want people to see themselves reflected in the brand."

How hard was it to make this enormous change in an iconic global brand?

Kim felt that Ruth Handler created the doll with a clear human truth at her core that will endure: a girl can be anything she wants to be.

Kim said, "Barbie is, and always has been, a revolutionary brand. We have to be reflective of the consumers who are shopping for her today, and then there's no stopping Barbie."

ABOVE: One of Mattel's career dolls was the Barbie 60th Anniversary Pilot Doll, released in 2019, dressed in a blue pilot's uniform with a matching pilot's cap and black boots. **FOLLOWING**: In 2016, Mattel introduced Barbie dolls who had diverse body types with new shapes and sizes for Barbie and friends, including petite, tall, thin, and curvy.

chapter 5

BARBIE LIFESTYLE

Barbie's first fans were quick to let Mattel know that they wanted Barbie to have a friend. There were thousands of letters specifically asking for a boyfriend. This made perfect sense to Ruth. She had seen her own daughter playing with both female and male paper dolls.

The late 1950s and early 1960s were a time marked by high expectations for home and family. On television, families watched *Father Knows Best, The Adventures of Ozzie and Harriet,* and *Dennis the Menace,* all modeling traditional families of the time. The women on these shows, up to any challenge, had equally great husbands. Surely, children would buy a male doll to go with Barbie.

But once again, toy buyers did not embrace the idea of a male doll. Boy dolls did not have a good sales history, and the buyers didn't believe that Barbie's success would transfer to an adult male doll.

In characteristic fashion, Ruth moved ahead despite the doubters. But she almost stumbled on an obvious hurdle. It was one thing to give Barbie breasts, but should Ken be anatomically correct? She thought there should be a suggestion of male anatomy, a bulge, however slight. Charlotte Johnson, who would expand her clothes designs to the new doll, agreed with Ruth. But the male design team pushed back, wanting no hint of genitalia at all.

Ruth accused them of having no guts.

Prototypes were ordered with varying degrees of a bulge that would show in underwear. Reluctantly, Ruth gave in to the research-and-design team's concerns that a doll that was anything less than neutered would hurt Mattel. In the end, the doll's crotch area was as flat as his stomach.

OPPOSITE: Ruth Handler with a collection of Barbie and Ken dolls from the early 1960s.

ABOVE LEFT: The original Bathing Suit Barbie and Ken from 1959. TOP RIGHT: From a 1960 Mattel advertisement showing a young girl smiling at a collection with Barbie, Ken, and their friends. BOTTOM RIGHT: A 1963 advertisement for Barbie and Ken's Hot Rod and Sports Car, built to fit the Barbie, Ken, and Midge dolls.

Ken debuted on March 11, 1961, at the American Toy Fair. He had the barest hint of a smile, better for children to imagine his personality and moods. He came with blond or brunette hair that was made of felt, but it rubbed off easily, especially when wet, and was soon replaced with plastic hair molded to his head. He wouldn't get rooted hair like Barbie until 1973. Sandals with a red strap matched his red trunks, and he carried a yellow terry cloth towel. Like Barbie, he was ready for many outfits.

Ken, named for Ruth's son, was introduced in the Mattel catalog with the tag line "He's a doll!" Barbie was a "Teen-age Fashion Model," but Ken's description was "Barbie's Boyfriend." He was 12 inches tall, and his television debut came in a commercial where he appeared in a ballroom. The commercial told the story of Barbie and Ken's relationship starting "at the dance," where Barbie "knew that she and Ken would be going together." Their coordinated outfits could be used for outings at the beach, fraternity dances, or even a wedding. Barbie's Wedding Day Set included a blue garter, and Ken's Tuxedo had a white boutonniere. As with Charlotte Johnson's Barbie clothes, Ken's outfits had all the precision, quality, and detail that buyers had come to expect.

According to her growing number of fans, Barbie needed a female friend too, and in 1963, freckle-faced Midge Hadley went on sale. Midge was Barbie's best friend and would later marry Allan, introduced in 1964. That same year, Barbie got a younger teenage sister named Skipper and Skipper got a friend named Skooter. Barbie's family really grew the next year when the preschool-age twins, Tutti and Todd, were introduced. And in 1966, Barbie got a cousin named Francie.

By 1968, Barbie had her first African American friend, Christie. She was part of a talking dolls group, each programmed to say short phrases that varied by doll. In a nod to the British Invasion, Stacey, a friend of Barbie's from the United Kingdom, also arrived in 1968. In her talking version, she had a British accent, and she was only made for three years. Her face sculpt would later be used for Malibu Barbie. And in recognition of the hippie era, hip and mod PJ was introduced in 1969, with beaded ties on her pigtails.

ABOVE: Talking Christie, the first African American Barbie doll, was introduced in 1968. The Christie doll shown here is from 1970, and wears a yellow-and-orange print top with orange vinyl trim and orange vinyl shorts.

ABOVE: Twiggy was a cultural icon and prominent teenage model in the 1960s, and Mattel released the Twiggy doll at the height of her career. Shown here is an advertisement from Mattel's 1968 catalog.

The 1960s also saw the first celebrity Barbie. Supermodel Twiggy went on sale in 1967 in a vertical-striped minidress and yellow boots. She was advertised as "London's top teen model."

Barbie's family didn't grow again until 1989, when her cousin Jazzie was introduced. Then, in 1992, Mattel introduced Barbie's sister, Stacie (not to be confused with her British friend Stacey from 1968). In 1995, Kelly (called Shelly in Europe) entered the scene. Kelly went out of production, and Chelsea took her place in 2011 as Barbie's youngest sister.

Over the decades, Barbie's world grew exponentially, but the thread that binds the dolls together is their relationships. Some relationships are part of the doll, like Barbie's family and friends, and some are relationships built through the potential play value of the various dolls.

Creating dolls that expand Barbie's world and girls' imaginations starts with a combined team from the Marketing, Design, and Public Relations departments. They brainstorm together about dolls that will be topical, like the recent Barbie Robotics Engineer and Game Developer dolls. They consider whether the doll will have global resonance, the age at which girls will understand the doll's given role, if the doll will serve a purpose, and whether it's a doll that can have great play value. For instance, the Robotics Engineer comes with a purple laptop and a tiny silver robot begging to be "activated."

Robert Best explained, "We're taking the path of Ruth's promise. We know that girls have a dream gap. Girls don't see themselves in society in as full a way as they can. So it's even more important for us to push that conversation. Yes, Barbie is a fashion doll, but Ruth Handler fought to get this doll out into the world. We have to reflect her fight. It's critical to raise women up and support that with the brand, because we have such a big megaphone."

In 2019, the career line introduced a partnership with *National Geographic*. Along with the Beekeeper Barbie and Butterfly Scientist were dolls that expanded on the idea of being a naturalist. There's a biologist, a conservationist, a

ABOVE: A vintage Twiggy doll, dressed in the "Turnouts" outfit from 1967, which consisted of a minidress with a striped multicolor bodice and silvertone skirt, accented with a wide silver belt at the hip, and silver boots.

photojournalist, and an astrophysicist, all with intriguing accessories. As Robert Best said, "We give girls what they want, but we also help them stretch their dreams. We pick jobs that girls will relate to."

Key to the Barbie message is showing careers where women are underrepresented. They call the concept "See It/Be It," and girls and their parents love the dolls. All the career dolls fit seamlessly into the world of Barbie. Barbie has become a "system of play," where her dimensions fit together. A mermaid might be found in Barbie's convertible, or a princess in a doctor's coat and stethoscope. Barbie embraces difference.

Storytelling packs with accessories allow the dolls to have adventures, like going to the movies, traveling, being a student, or having a day at the beach.

Barbie's Dreamhouse and accessories have also evolved to accommodate her growing circle. The Barbie Dreamhouse used to be designed just for her, but now it has expanded rooms, beds, and even bunkbeds, and invites a constellation of dolls for play. Barbie cars and campers have also grown to include more characters.

Barbie's family is about relationships and connection. Her three sisters are important to her. Chelsea, the youngest, needs support, but also has a budding personality. Skipper, a young teen, and Stacey, barely an adolescent, offer a full range of play. Nurturing is a popular play pattern, so Skipper is a babysitter. With her own babysitting business, she also encourages the idea of female entrepreneurship.

Barbie also has friends outside of the day-to-day world. Her Dreamtopia line includes mermaids, fairies, and princesses, plus MerBears and Unicorns. These fantasy archetypes have light and sound, but they also have different body types. In Barbie's world, even fantastical play incorporates inclusion and diversity. Fairies with gossamer wings and mermaids with rainbow tails still reflect the wide range of children who play with them.

With every incarnation and every new doll that launches, Barbie is sending her thematic message: girls can be anything.

ABOVE: Barbie's space career began in 1965 when Mattel released Miss Astronaut Barbie and Mr. Astronaut Ken doll. Shown here is the 1985 Astronaut Barbie doll, in fashion with the time, dressed in a fuchsia and silver metallic bodysuit top, matching pants with a silver belt, and pink over-the-knee boots.

ABOVE: The Barbie lifestyle expanded in various directions. In 1966, surfing was all the rage, and Barbie and friends were part of it. Shown here is a Mattel advertisement from 1966 for "The Active World of Barbie," with Barbie, Ken, and Skipper riding the wave. FOLLOWING: Ruth and Elliot Handler with their Barbie and friends lifestyle display at the Canada Toy Show in 1971.

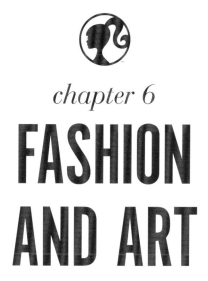

chapter 6

FASHION AND ART

Barbie was destined from the start to have a beautiful wardrobe. She was the brainchild of Ruth Handler, and Ruth loved fashion. Ruth's first Barbie clothing designer, Charlotte Johnson, also loved style and fashion.

There were twenty-two outfits in Barbie's inaugural collection, including a satin bridal gown with tulle, a jacket with matching sheath skirts reminiscent of Chanel, the red-and-white stripes of a travel ensemble with a dark blue pencil skirt called Roman Holiday, the fur stole and long white gloves of bubble-skirted Parisienne, and underclothes that girls might not yet be using, but could anticipate, including a bra and a slip, baby doll pajamas, and a full-length negligee and peignoir.

Outfits like Resort Set, Suburban Shopper, and Saturday Matinee were all popular with young girls. Ruth wanted to be sure that Barbie could also dress for common activities, like going to prom, a football game, or working at a job.

Charlotte started by using the "TPO" method of design. *T* for the time of day when a fashion piece would be worn, *P* for the place Barbie would wear the clothing, and *O* for the occasion where the fashion would be worn.

Although lingerie was designed for Barbie in the initial line, Charlotte decided that there was little play value in underwear, and that a bathing suit would offer more opportunity and imagination. That's why tens of thousands of Barbie dolls would first be seen dressed for a dip in the pool or ocean.

Charlotte's initial inspiration for Barbie's clothes came from *Vogue* magazine, as well as *Vogue* sewing patterns, where the pictures on the covers gave her ideas. She had

---

OPPOSITE: Artist and fashion designer BillyBoy* posing with one of his dolls. He had a collection of more than eleven thousand Barbie dolls and three thousand Ken dolls. He also authored the 1987 book *Barbie: Her Life and Times*. From 1984–90, Mattel sponsored two fashion tours curated by BillyBoy*, and later he worked as both a designer and consultant for Mattel, where he designed two Barbie dolls.

to think of everything, like creating a stuffed dog to go with Barbie's negligee and the pink plastic hand mirror with Barbie's logo on the back. Charlotte would be known simply as "CJ" on the boxes that held her creations.

Charlotte relied heavily on her knowledge of production and her understanding of how clothes could be constructed. She was on the lookout for simplicity in sewing design. For instance, the bathing suit was composed of only two darts and one seam. Barbie's clothes were die cut, so Charlotte could be sure of the precision. Bradley Justice, an expert on Charlotte Johnson, has taken apart every outfit from 1959 to understand how they were made. He said, "There was magic in Charlotte's pattern-making and skill."

Detail was always important. Twinsets were very popular in the 1950s. Charlotte found a Japanese knitting factory to make the sweaters. The first order was for two hundred and fifty thousand, before Ruth knew whether Barbie would even sell! They sold so well, they had to be reordered.

Barbie's original silk flowers came from a legendary Japanese silk flower maker, Hiroshi Fukushima. For all the tiny zippers, Charlotte found YKK, a zipper manufacturer. It was the first time they had made zippers that were size 0. The fun of using those miniature zippers led to many letters from little girls wanting more!

The first twenty-two designs were modern and cutting edge, and still maintained a 1950s flavor while also anticipating the 1960s. Some people think the first Barbie clothes were inspired by Jackie Kennedy, but she was not yet well known. Bradley Justice joked, "Maybe Jackie copied Barbie."

ABOVE: A Barbie look alike poses next to the new Barbie U.S. postage stamp in El Segundo, California, on August 24, 1999. As Barbie celebrated her 40th anniversary, the stamp was one of the winners in a public vote in a series celebrating the 20th century.

ABOVE: Mbili Barbie, released in 2002, as part of Mattel's innovative Treasures of Africa Collection created by New York designer Byron Lars. She is dressed in a ribbed corset of multi-colored beads accenting her intricately woven, backless sweater; a skirt featuring a ruffled waist and shirred V-line design, a full bustle is composed of ostrich feathers, and Azure blue boots.

TOP: Famous French hairdresser Louis Alexandre Raimon, known as Alexandre de Paris, styles Barbie's hair in Paris on November 25, 1993. BOTTOM: Bloomingdale's and Mattel present one-of-a-kind *Hairspray* Ken and Barbie dolls, with Ken as Edna Turnblad and Barbie as Tracy Turnblad.

ABOVE: Jewelry designer Tarina Tarantino arrives at "The Pink Plastic Party of the Year" to celebrate the launch of the Tarina Tarantino Barbie doll and jewelry collection, at the Tarina Tarantino Boutique on July 17, 2008, in Los Angeles, California.

Under the years of Charlotte's direction, both in Japan and California, Mattel became the largest manufacturer of women's apparel.

After twenty years at the top of fashion design for Mattel, Charlotte was honored with a gilded Barbie doll. She had not only dressed Barbie, but also Barbie's friends, family, and special dolls like Miss America. "We make miniature fashions, not doll clothes," Charlotte told a reporter. At the award ceremony, Ruth said, "Many could have done what Charlotte did, but no one could have done it better."

Charlotte's work not only became collectible, it inspired countless designers and seamstresses like her.

Abby Glassenberg wrote a column for *Sew News* magazine called "The Common Thread." In it, she talked about how sewing becomes part of our lives. "As an adult who writes about sewing and is involved in the sewing community every day, I noticed that it seemed most people started sewing because they sewed for Barbie. Barbie was like a mannequin, a miniature woman, so with a paper towel you could drape a gown and make Barbie haute couture, because she had breasts and hips and long legs, like a fashion model."

Abby continued, "Barbie really plays a role as a muse for sewing. She's so accessible, and so small and easy to hold, so even with a small amount of fabric or even Kleenex, or a necktie, you can make her a hat or a dress. She's like a canvas that gives you permission to design for her."

ABOVE: Actress Angela Griffin (left) and Angela Rippon (right), Chairman of English National Ballet, pose in 2001 with a Barbie doll in London, when it was announced that the English National Ballet had signed a sponsorship deal with Mattel to stage Tchaikovsky's *The Nutcracker*.

Major designers remember starting with Barbie as well. Anna Sui recalled, "I started dressing Barbie dolls with my own designs at an early age." Cynthia Rowley added, "As a little girl, I spent countless hours playing with my Barbie dolls, even designing and sewing one of a kind outfits for the doll. I guess you could say Barbie gave me my start as a designer." Jason Wu, designer for celebrities, first realized his love of fashion designing for Barbie dolls. He had more than a hundred Barbies that he used for styling hair. These designers, and more, have created fashions for the Barbie market.

Jeremy Scott gave the world eye-popping designs for many pop stars, including Britney Spears, Miley Cyrus, and Katy Perry. His limited-edition Moschino Barbie, with a bright and prominent display of gold bling, was the subject of a first-ever ad for Barbie that featured a little boy.

Jeremy told the *New Yorker* that he was thrilled. "It's not a fashion story—it's a news story . . . I've done something that's affecting culture. The thing I love most about Barbie is that she is the ultimate muse. She's worn every style and design imaginable and at the same time she's had every possible profession you can dream of."

Barbie has also adapted with the political and cultural changes throughout time. The upheavals of the 1960s sent every part of America racing toward change. Civil rights, women's rights, and anti-Vietnam war movements shook the country and inspired young people to question authority. *Rolling Stone* magazine began publishing just in time for the Woodstock music festival in 1969, which cemented the hippie lifestyle in the American mind.

By the late 1960s, Barbie got "mod" clothes, following the miniskirt craze that came out of English designer Mary Quant's fashion house. Pairing the skirt with go-go boots, the Barbie Zokko! outfit was sold in 1967. With its shimmery silver sleeveless top, bright blue-teal skirt, and splash-of-

LEFT: Japanese ballerina Erena Takahashi, who at 23 was the youngest principal dancer of the English National Ballet, in London, 2001. **RIGHT**: Mattel's Nutcracker Barbie, released in 2001.

ABOVE: Posing on the stairs by her Beverly Hills home, actress and model Corazon Ugalde Yellen Armenta wears an outfit identical to her collector's Barbie doll—an outfit called "Matinee Fashion" from 1965. Armenta had her attire specially made for wearing to Barbie doll convention fashion shows.

ABOVE: This image shows custom Barbie Jewelry designed for a 2003 collection to be sold by auction to benefit the French Red Cross, on December 11, 2003, in Paris, France. This Mikimoto Barbie is dressed in clothes designed by Nina Ricci, including pink crepe silk dress. Barbie is wearing ear pendants, a necklace, and a navel piece made of yellow gold with cultured pearls, and the bracelet is a string of Mikimoto cultured pearls.

orange waistband, matched with orange dangly earrings, Barbie left the 1950s behind.

Then came the 1970s with the first Starbucks opening in Seattle, creating a common space for social meetings that would bloom everywhere in the country. Early personal computers, email, video games, and floppy discs hinted at the new future of technology. Cable television began reaching America's screens.

People talked about a sexual revolution changing society's attitudes toward marriage, divorce, and LGBTQ+ rights. A "second wave" of the women's movement had brought feminism to the forefront, with calls for women's equality. Women were given the right to choose to have an abortion, birth control pills became more available, and the first test-tube baby was born.

Barbie leapt into the new freedom, capturing the spirit of the 1970s, with outfits like Flower Wower, with splotches of overlapping psychedelic flowers and bright green shoes. Maxi 'n Midi, with its belted coat of blue foil fabric and fluffy blue fur over a striped dress and knee-high boots; and Gypsy Spirit, with its pink chiffon blouse and blue-and-gold vest and skirt. Barbie even had

ABOVE: The Gianmaria Buccellati Barbie is wearing fashion designed by Michael Kors, including a gray cashmere jersey dress with a gray and anthracite chinchilla stole. Barbie's jewelry, designed by Buccellati, is dual-gold engraved "Primavera" necklace, earrings, and bracelet, encrusted with diamonds and rubies. The Barbie Jewelry 2003 Collection was auctioned on December 11, 2003, in Paris, France, to benefit the French Red Cross.

ABOVE: A model walks the runway during the *Barbie by Cigdem Akin* show during Mercedes-Benz Istanbul Fashion Week at Zorlu Performance Hall on October 11, 2019 in Istanbul, Turkey.

a peasant blouse, while Ken had a fringed leather vest. For her sixteenth birthday, Barbie got a special-edition T-shirt-and-jeans outfit.

But Barbie maintained her glamorous tradition as well. In 1977, Superstar Barbie appeared. With her pink, satin low-cut dress, matching boa, strappy shoes, and star-shaped stand, Superstar Barbie had a teeth-flashing smile and higher-looking cheekbones. She was destined to be a bestseller for many years.

The 1980s saw Michael Jackson take over the music world with his album *Thriller*, and Madonna created a sensation with her debut album. MTV was launched, as were McDonald's McNuggets. Children discovered Nintendo and *The Simpsons*. America continued to explore the universe with a successful space shuttle launch and a fatal mission by the *Columbia* to repair an orbiting satellite.

In form and fashion, Barbie took the lead in the 1980s, with an astronaut uniform that included a space helmet. Barbie and the Rockers met the "girl band" moment, hitting the stage with sparkles, shine, shimmer, and microphones. By her thirtieth birthday, in 1989, she was ready to celebrate

TOP: Mattel featured an extended line of Barbie figures emphasizing themes of haute couture, Hollywood, and celebrity—including this Marilyn Monroe Giftset Barbie—at the International Toy Fair February in New York on February 10, 2002. **BOTTOM**: Fashion Bloggers Cailli Beckerman (left) and Sam Beckerman (right), who is wearing a Moschino Barbie sweater, during Art Basel in Miami Beach on December 6, 2014.

her Pink Jubilee at New York's Lincoln Center. She had a full wardrobe for her growing list of careers, including a day-to-night outfit that could transform from a business suit to a glittering pink dress for a night on the town.

The 1980s also saw the first designer partnership. The Barbie brand collaborated with Oscar de la Renta to create four outfits in one package, which included three dresses for the red carpet and one pantsuit. And eight years after the first Barbie collector's convention, the 1988 Holiday Barbie started a tradition of glamorous collectible Barbie dolls.

Andy Warhol cemented the connection between Barbie and popular culture with his iconic image of Barbie's face. After Warhol painted Elvis, Marilyn Monroe, and Mickey Mouse. His muse, the jewelry designer called BillyBoy* (spelled with an asterisk), inspired him to paint Barbie.

Warhol had wanted to paint BillyBoy*, but he refused to cooperate and instead suggested Warhol paint BillyBoy*'s obsession—Barbie. Warhol used one of Billy Boy*'s tens of thousands of Barbie dolls as a model and called the painting *Portrait of BillyBoy*.

Later, BillyBoy* designed two Barbie dolls for Mattel, the Le Nouveau Theatre de la Mode doll, and the Feelin'

TOP: Dominican American fashion designer Oscar de la Renta (center) poses with models in fashions designed for Mattel's Barbie dolls, at a Barbie Fashion Show in 1984.
BOTTOM: Television host Hofit Golan poses at the Jeremy Scott & Moschino Party with Barbie in Miami Beach, Florida, on December 4, 2014.

ABOVE: A collection of Limited Edition Barbie dolls, dressed in stunning fashions from two of the world's premiere designers. From left to right are the Christian Dior Barbie Doll, released in 1997; the Bob Mackie Gold Barbie doll, released in 1990; and the Christian Dior Barbie Doll, released in 1995.

ABOVE: The Stephen Burrows Pazette Barbie Doll was designed by Linda Kyaw and released in 2012 as part of Mattel's Gold Label line of Barbie dolls. The show-stopping doll was dressed in an extraordinary ensemble, including silvery glitter, rhinestones, and sequins. Her silver-colored headpiece features a cascade of white feathers.

Groovy doll. And for the first time, Mattel put the designer's name on the box. In 2014, BillyBoy* sold the Warhol Barbie painting for $1,161,780.

As Barbie continued her popularity in the 1990s, America was introduced to Amazon.com, Harry Potter, and the early web-based email service Hotmail. Britney Spears burst onto the music scene, while *Survivor* and *Buffy the Vampire Slayer* captivated television viewers.

For Barbie, the decade was marked by recognition of the amazing designers who continued to create her astonishing wardrobe, including Carol Spencer, Robert Best, Janet Goldblatt, Kitty Black-Perkins, Ann Driskill, Abbe Littleton, Monique Lhuillier, Anna Sui, and Cynthia Rowley, plus the designers who, like Barbie, are recognizable by one name: Calvin, Cartier, Gucci, Versace, and Vera.

ABOVE: Mattel celebrates forty-five years of Barbie fashion with a runway display featuring Barbies with clothes by designers such as Versace, Kate Spade, and Bob Mackie at the Mattel booth at Toy Fair in New York City, February 15, 2004.

ABOVE: Artist Andy Warhol displays his portrait of a Barbie doll in New York on February 10, 1986.

ABOVE: Models display iconic Barbie outfits in the Barbie Runway Show during the 2009 Mercedes Benz Fashion Week in New York City, February 14, 2009.

ABOVE: More than 700 Barbie dolls were displayed during the exhibition *Barbie, life of an icon* at the Museum of Decorative Arts as part of the Paris Fashion Week Womenswear Fall/Winter 2016/2017 on March 9, 2016 in Paris, France.

In 1990, Bob Mackie became the first of many famous designers to collaborate with the Barbie brand on a collector doll. His Gold Barbie featured five thousand hand-sewn golden sequins on a form-fitting, full-length gown with a crisscross bodice.

The 2000s saw hip-hop become part of the Rock and Roll Hall of Fame and a woman make two serious attempts at the presidency. Reality television and superhero films found popularity. Fashion often looked back to the '60s, '70s, and '80s, including velour tracksuits and tapered pants.

For Barbie, more fashion collaborations were in store. A doll and shoe collection was created by Christian Louboutin. Fine jewelry called Barbie Rocks came from the design team of Layna and Alan Friedman. Coach got into Barbie's world with mini leather bags designed just for her. And when Barbie's foot was redesigned so that it could go to a flat position, Sophia Webster designed a line of shoes for her new, flexible feet.

In 2009, for Barbie's fiftieth birthday, fifty-one designers created looks for Barbie's first ever runway show, held at New York's Mercedes-Benz Fashion Week. From Donna Karan and Tommy Hilfiger, Diane von Furstenberg to Bob Mackie, the show opened with magnificent pink curtains drawing aside to reveal a model dressed as the Number One Barbie, in her original bathing suit, with a large blonde ponytail. The collection was described as "surreal" and included Ken in a black velvet jacket and jeans. The fabulous show, which drew screams of delight from mothers and daughters in the audience, moved on to a celebration at London Fashion Week that included the young designers Roksanda Ilincic and Danielle Scutt.

LEFT: Singer Cyndi Lauper poses with Barbie and Pooch the Pup at the unveiling of the "Ultimate Toy Catalog" at FAO Schwartz in New York City on October 10, 2001. The show benefited New Yorkers for Children's programs that help New York City children affected by the events of 9/11. **RIGHT**: Mattel and Ford join forces as both Barbie and the Mustang celebrate their 40th birthday at an event in Southern California on April 20, 1999.

TOP: Some of the fifty blonde participants who entered a Barbie look alike contest outside of Hotel Russell in London on January 17, 1991. BOTTOM: Adriana Karembeu, Ambassador of the French Red Cross, poses next to the 2003 Barbie jewelry collection in Paris, where top jewelers got together to dress up a collection of Barbie dolls to be auctioned for the Red Cross, on December 18, 2003.

ABOVE: The late designer Karl Lagerfeld with the Barbie doll made in his likeness, in 2014.

ABOVE: The Karl Lagerfeld Barbie doll, released in 2014, inspired by the designer's signature style, with elements borrowed from the Karl Lagerfeld line and Karl's iconic silhouette. The doll is dressed in a tailored black jacket, white high-collared men's shirt with French cuffs, black satin cravat, and fitted black jeans. Accessories include black fingerless gloves, a zippered handbag, and sunglasses.

ABOVE: Model, cover girl, and pageant-winner Corazon Ugalde Yellen Armenta poses in custom-made outfits modeled after Barbie fashions.

ABOVE: Young models celebrating with designer Bettina Liano on the runway at the fashion launch for Barbie by Bettina Liano in Melbourne, Australia, on September 21, 2005.

Barbie was captivating and compelling as a doll, and with her extraordinary fashions she becomes something more: an icon that invites imagination through not only playing with her or collecting her, but even *being* her.

Robert Best was thoughtful about the history of Barbie fashion and his role in it. "I love having my name on dolls because I'm passionate about the doll, and I want to be part of the great legacy. I'm part of the change, and the new guard. Collectors are aware of the history of Ruth Handler and Charlotte Johnson, and I'm the extension of that great tradition. We have younger designers who will take over from me. All of us are letting consumers know that we're listening."

One consumer and fan has brought the Barbie design into real life. Corazon Ugalde Yellen Armenta, known simply as Cora, was born and raised in the Philippines, where she didn't have a Barbie. She loved to play with fashion dolls, and after she came to the United States and had her daughter, she started buying Barbie dolls.

"I was a model and actress," Cora explained, "and did a beauty and fitness book, *Total Beauty in Life, the Natural Way.* So, I loved Barbie because she was the ultimate fashion model."

Cora became Mrs. Philippines 2018, and she competed for Mrs. Asia 2018. In the 1990s, she modeled for many

---

ABOVE: Models pose at Barbie's Dream Closet during Mercedez-Benz Fashion Week at the Lincoln Center, New York City, in February 2012. Here, fans could step into one of several "closets" and, through augmented reality, virtually try on various Barbie outfits.

ABOVE: Barbie doll look alikes prepare to embark on a tour around the UK to meet thousands of fans. The ten real-life Barbies were all set to launch the country's biggest-ever Barbie event, at the Woolworth's store in London, on October 19, 2000.

designers, including Lanvin and Yves Saint Laurent. She's also been an actress on television and on stage. Cora was dubbed a Living Doll Barbie after modeling several life-size Barbie fashions through the years for Barbie Conventions' fashion shows! As Cora said, "I feel like I did everything too, lots of careers and experiences, like Barbie."

Cora founded the Beverly Hills Barbie Club but keeps her collection of more than a thousand Barbie dolls, as well as other dolls, in her Las Vegas home. She said, "I love that Barbie can do anything and has so many careers. She's an American icon."

Lisa McKnight, Executive Vice President and Chief Brand Officer of Mattel, has been in charge of the Barbie lifestyle—everything that is Barbie around the world. She said, "I loved Barbie when I was young, and I played with her along with my younger sister. I was fascinated with being the older girl and played out being a babysitter because a babysitter could drive a car and have a boyfriend." McKnight laughed. "I also liked being a teacher, and I was an athlete. I played soccer, so Malibu Barbie was a favorite."

It was around 2008 when Mattel "honed in on the notion that through Barbie, a girl can be whatever she wants to be. We've become maniacally focused on why Ruth Handler created Barbie. She knew there was a dream gap for girls, and there still is."

ABOVE: The Barbie Fashion Designer Collection Launch by Bettina Liano fashion parade in Australia starred twenty-five young girls, on September 21, 2005.

McKnight and her team looked at what Barbie inspires and enables beyond the doll. "She's more than a doll," McKnight said, "but the doll started it all, and we've extended and expanded the brand. The culture and society embrace Barbie, and Barbie is also part of the culture. We're showing girls Shero and Inspiring Women dolls. If you can't see it, you can't be it."

What keeps Barbie culturally relevant? McKnight added, "There's this wonderful open-endedness to Barbie. She's a canvas for storytelling."

They can wake up on Barbie sheets in Barbie pajamas, brush their teeth with a Barbie toothbrush, slip on a branded backpack and sneakers, before heading to school with their Barbie lunchbox. After school, how about a Barbie licensed manicure and a spin around the block in Barbie themed inline skates? Bath time finds many Barbie products to use. Then back to bed under a Barbie comforter, comfortably sleeping in the shadow of a Dreamhouse and shelves full of dolls. And if that's not enough, Barbie appears on screens as well, with shows, movies, a YouTube channel, and a variety of apps.

According to McKnight, "Most toys have three- to five-year life cycles, so she is unique in the toy industry. Barbie stands the test of time. Everyone has their Barbie story."

ABOVE: Ten-year-old Olga Bagiotas from Prahan, Australia, with Barbie on the catwalk during the Barbie by Bettina Liano Designer Collection Star Search casting session in Australia, on July 7, 2005. **FOLLOWING**: Models on the catwalk wearing designer dresses to be auctioned at the Barbie 45th Anniversary Fashion Show to benefit the French Red Cross and Child AIDS Program in Africa, on March 9, 2004.

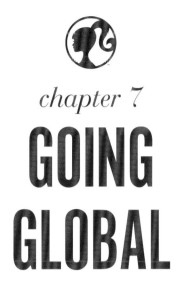

chapter 7

GOING GLOBAL

Barbie has been a global phenomenon for decades. From Asia to the Middle East, from Australia to Alaska, children allow their imaginations to build new adventures for the many toys that are part of the Barbie brand.

There is a world of technology connecting Barbie fans across continents and oceans.

Shortly after the first Barbie went on sale, Dell Comics began a series of comic books called *Barbie and Ken*. Readers were invited to travel along as the duo went to Europe, played tennis, made an appearance onstage, and had other adventures. There was also the bimonthly *Barbie* magazine, with features like how to grow a salad, babysitting, and making a paper dress.

The magazine also had a series on girls around the world with titles like, "If You Were an Irish Girl" and "If You Were an Israeli Girl." Through the magazine, girls learned that Barbie's father was George Roberts, and her mother was Margaret. She had a sister named Skipper, and Midge had a brother named Albert.

There was also a Barbie fan club, which grew exponentially throughout Barbie's first decade, without the advantage of social media. But as the Internet took hold, chat rooms popped up dedicated to the Barbie brand, and websites allowed fans and collectors to broadcast their ideas for Barbie, her friends, her fashions, and her larger world of houses and accessories.

Today, Barbie has a Facebook page, Instagram accounts, X (formerly Twitter), YouTube, and TikTok accounts. She's captured social media.

An exciting global event happened in 2016. There was an exhibition at the Musée des Arts Décoratifs at the Palais du Louvre in Paris, France. Under triple arches, at the top of a broad marble staircase, a solid pink wall announced "Barbie." Inside, seven hundred Barbie dolls were displayed.

OPPOSITE: Mattel features the *Legally Blonde 2* collection at the 2003 Toy Fair in New York City on February 16, 2003.

The innovative arrangements of dolls showed Barbie's more than two dozen hair colors, her fourteen skin tones, and her new shapes and sizes.

Anne Monier, curator of the Louvre's Toy Department, told National Public Radio, "Beauty is also about diversity. And today, you cannot give a child one doll and say, this is a beautiful doll. You need to show the child different models of beauty so that they can pick the one that they want to identify with."

The museum included works from their collection of dolls and gowns, as well as works by contemporary artists, and a full spectrum of media exhibits that show how the world has changed.

Perhaps there's no better testimony to Barbie's massive reach than the dedication of fans across the globe. A few collectors have caught the world's attention. Devoted to Barbie in their own special way, they discover their creative expression and their love for helping others through her inspiration.

Jian Yang lives in the Bartley neighborhood of Singapore. In his gleaming white apartment, thousands of Barbie dolls, neatly lined up, sit on the shelves that cover his living-room walls. They frame his television with a kaleidoscope of color, an entertaining reminder of his fascination with Barbie.

Jian has been in the advertising business for nearly twenty years, and for all that time, and longer, Barbie dolls have captivated him.

Jian's introduction to Barbie came in 1984 when he was five years old. He couldn't read the names on the presents under the Christmas tree, so he opened a present meant for his two-year-old sister. It was a Great Shape Barbie in a turquoise leotard and matching headband, and he loved it. After that, he was gifted his own. "I got Dream Glow Barbie," Jian said. "She had

ABOVE: Another view of the more than 700 Barbie dolls displayed during the exhibition *Barbie, life of an icon* at the Museum of Decorative Arts as part of Paris Fashion Week on March 9, 2016.

ABOVE: Collector and artist Jian Yang from Singapore poses with a small selection of Barbie dolls from his huge collection of more than twelve thousand dolls sourced from fifty different countries.

ABOVE: An assortment of Jian Yang's fashions that he creates while traveling using various forms of paper products, including toilet paper, napkins, and tissue.

glow-in-the-dark stars on her dress, so I'd crawl under the bed and watch her glow."

He started getting an allowance in his teens and used the money to buy more dolls and clothes. "As a teenager, the boy toys went away, but I kept my Barbies. I never really played imaginary games or made up stories with Barbie. To me, she was an iconic illustration. She was like a drawing that came to life."

Jian does not like to call himself a "collector," since his incentive for getting dolls is not to complete a certain series and he doesn't buy dolls to sell them. "I've always been a very private collector. I always just figured I was a boy who played with toys, and one of those toys happened to be Barbie. I'm very visual, so when I see a doll I like, I decide if I want it."

And he has discovered a wonderfully creative side to himself—the creation of Barbie clothes from tissue, toilet paper, and napkins. Jian's paper Barbie wardrobe is fragile, astonishing, and mesmerizing. It's difficult to imagine how he can create such intricate dresses, hats, and flowers with such delicate material.

As for how he started making these fabulous designs, Jian said, "I was sent to Colombo, Sri Lanka, by my company. I stayed at this big hotel on the edge of Colombo by the sea. There was nothing around the hotel, and nothing to do, and I was stuck there every night. One day, I bought a Barbie doll in Colombo. As I sat in the hotel, I realized I had some tape in my toiletry bag and some manicure scissors, and of course, there was toilet paper in the bathroom. So, I sat on the toilet and made a rosette. I always liked to fiddle with stuff, so I randomly rolled the toilet paper and thought, 'Hey, a rose.'" That was Jian's first creation, but he wasn't satisfied with it, so he made another.

For the next two weeks, he made a rosette every night. He put the best one on Instagram, and it got positive responses, so he made more. Soon, he branched out to dresses, everything from sleek strapless evening gowns to a dirndl-skirted party dress, and imaginative hats, all made from white tissue.

Jian only does tissue creations when he travels. "It's an interesting way to document my travel because I use

ABOVE: Collector and artist Jian Yang poses with a vintage Number One blonde ponytail Barbie doll in front of his pristine collection at his home in Singapore.

paper from where I am." He is starting to use napkins from restaurants he visits. "As a homeowner with lots of expenses, I need to save money, so that's why I use hotel toilet paper."

Jian still buys dolls. His new Barbie dolls arrive weekly in Amazon boxes. He's also listed in *Asia Book of Records* for having the largest collection in Asia. Why is he still amassing dolls? Jian explained, "I've been in advertising for a long time, and in advertising you have to be in tune with trends and pop culture. I see Barbie as a pop culture icon. For instance, the Misty Copeland doll introduced me to her story. I did my research, and now I'm deeply

knowledgeable about a pop culture icon who's indicative of celebrity. Barbie tells the world's story through one medium, which is the toy."

Even though Jian travels for his work and has seen a lot of the world, he believes Barbie lets him see even more.

"With Barbie I see all the consumer touch-points and how a market is built. I like the creation of Barbie's fictional universe, which isn't bound by stereotypes that might be held about people in the Middle East, or Americans, or Asians. I'll never get rid of my dolls. Barbie will always be that icon. She's forever, certainly as a part of history."

ABOVE: A young model walks down the runway during the "Barbie Featuring the Pink Dolls" portion of the Macy's Passport Gala to Benefit HIV/AIDS Research and Awareness in Santa Monica, California, on September 30, 2004.

How many stories can Barbie tell? In Australia, a Barbie fan is answering that question on her own YouTube channel.

When she was twelve years old, Grace Mulgrew had more than a hundred Barbie dolls. She always liked to act out Barbie stories when she played by herself or with her cousins. "I thought it would be cool to see one of my own videos up there with the other Barbie videos." One day, she asked her father to videotape her.

In the video, Grace pretended to be her blonde Barbie as she showed viewers what's in the refrigerator, how the oven opens, and the airplane seat where Barbie's mother slept.

Grace talked almost nonstop, a little girl's voice showing the grown-up world of her house.

Greg put the video up on YouTube, and neither he nor Grace looked at it again. Then, about nine months later, Grace's cousin called with startling news. He told Grace that her video on YouTube was really popular. Grace said, "No, you have the wrong video." But when she looked on YouTube she found that her video had nine million views! Grace and Greg couldn't believe it, so they made another video.

In the second video, Grace pretended Barbie was a mother of twins. They were on a cruise ship with Ken. In

---

ABOVE: A collection of Barbie dolls from the exhibit *Barbie the Icon*, held at MUDEC (Museo delle Culture) in Milan, Italy, on February 10, 2016.

ABOVE: A canceled postage stamp celebrating Classic Toys from Australia with an image of a vintage 1962 Red Flare Barbie doll, circa 2009.

the story, they all fell into the water, went swimming, and got lost on a small sand island. The video got even more views than the first one. Greg said, "Kids didn't care about the quality [of the video]. They cared about the story. We planned out ahead what was going to happen with Barbie, but it wasn't scripted. It was like the camera wasn't even there." After about ten videos, Greg started using a green screen so Grace's hand and arm didn't show when Barbie was moved around.

Years later, Grace had more than a billion total views, and she had nearly three million subscribers to her YouTube channel, *Grace's World*. "We can see through Grace's videos how well Barbie is doing, and how kids are latching on to it every day as they come on to her channel," Greg said.

Thanks to Barbie, Greg and Grace have not only shared a rare father-daughter bond, but a business that relies on Grace's creativity and the doll she has always loved.

Grace is not alone in entertaining fans through social media. In Los Angeles, California, another fan shared her own love of Barbie. Azusa Yakamoto was born in Japan, where she had fashion dolls as a child, but Barbies were difficult to find. She finally received a Barbie lunchbox when she was fifteen years old. She said, "I was so unlucky when I was little, because I couldn't get a Barbie. But because of that, I never saw the doll as a little kid's toy."

Azusa loved her lunchbox, which looked "like cool American pop culture." Soon she was using the lunchbox as a purse. Around this time, Azusa became an exchange student in the little town of Bluffton, Indiana, where she lived on a farm for a year. She was delighted to be able to start collecting Barbie dolls. "I bought whatever I liked. My host family had kids who were fourteen and eleven and had already stopped playing with Barbie dolls. They made fun of my interest. But I didn't know why, because I didn't think Barbie was for kids."

Azusa returned to Japan, where she started selling Barbie-brand adult clothes, and bought more Barbie dolls. She was working hard and saving money to move to the United States. One of the reasons she wanted to move was because Barbie-brand items were very expensive in Japan.

TOP: Grace Mulgrew with her collection of Barbie dolls, 2019. **MIDDLE**: A screenshot from Episode 179, "The Karate Master," from *Grace's World*. **BOTTOM**: A screen shot from Episode 183, "The Imaginary Friend," from *Grace's World*.

When Azusa was thirty, she got a student visa to come to America. She began to do nail art. "I started designing Barbie nails to match Barbie fashions."

Today she has about 250 dolls, but it is Barbie-brand adult clothes and purses that make up the bulk of her collection. "I wear the clothes every day. That is my wardrobe. I only own Barbie shirts."

Manicuring is Azusa's main business, along with a YouTube channel called *Azusa Barbie*. The videos range from how to cook pink pasta, corn dogs, or popcorn, to watching Azusa's morning routine in her Barbie-themed apartment. She used five shades of pink to paint every room and filled the apartment with Barbie-brand items like pillows, teacups, and posters.

There are also plenty of do-it-yourself Barbie decorations, like the slatted blinds, a cabinet, and even the refrigerator. "I love DIY! I'm not just buying. I like creating by myself. When I think of something that I want with Barbie, if Mattel doesn't sell it, then I make it. I paint everything—walls, cabinets, floors—so it looks like Barbie's house. That's what Barbie tells us: we can be anything. Anything is possible. That's Barbie's attitude, so that's why I do it myself."

As a teenager she had a rare illness that required six surgeries. "That's what made me feel that I should do whatever I want to do," she said. "I learned early that life is fragile. I want to help kids, to do kids' nails, to donate Barbies. I want to help a million kids who are sick or poor."

Azusa's devotion to Barbie is stronger than ever. "I think Barbie's forever because she's not just a kid's fashion doll. She's a fashion item. She's not just a popular toy for one generation. She is totally a part of culture, and I love her."

ABOVE: Barbie's official Instagram page, @barbiestyle, has millions of followers. In this post from March 15, 2018, the Iris Apfel Barbie doll, modeled after the dynamic fashion icon, poses with Barbie, celebrating the release of her new book, *Iris Apfel: Accidental Icon.*

 barbiestyle ✔ • Follow
Marciano Art Foundation

barbiestyle Made it to
@marcianoartfoundation for the perfect
picture opp. The #KusamaxMAF exhibit
"With All My Love For The Tulips, I Pray
Forever (2011)" has me seeing spots! 🖤
#YayoiKusama #MAF #barbie
#barbiestyle

Load more comments

erica9876543210 @anoma_andy

barbie_fotos_anto 😀 🙂 🙂 🙂 🙂 🙂

creativewithdolls Love her art sooo! 😍

roselle_lie2 👰 🐒 🐒

♡ ☐ ⬆   ☐

31,385 likes

AUGUST 30

TOP LEFT: Image from Barbie's Instagram page, @barbiestyle, shows Barbie, Ashley Graham, and Ibtihaj Muhammad dolls at the *Glamour Magazine* Women of the Year Awards on November 13, 2017. **TOP RIGHT**: Barbie at Christian Siriano's show during New York Fashion Week on September 9, 2017. **BOTTOM**: Barbie visiting the Yayoi Kusama exhibit at the Marciano Art Foundation in Los Angeles on August 30, 2017.

ABOVE: Barbie blogger and collector Azusa Sakamoto—also known as Azusa Barbie—poses in her Barbie-themed home, which she has turned into a Barbie shrine, in West Hollywood, on December 12, 2018.

ABOVE: Azusa Yakamoto's real-life Barbie dreamhouse. Azusa is shown in her West Hollywood home on December 29, 2017. **FOLLOWING**: To celebrate the opening of their store in Miami Beach, Florida, Alchemist—a retailer whose mission is to bring together the synergetic world of fashion, design, and architecture—created a Barbie retrospective. The installation featured ten life-sized Barbie dolls dressed in custom Chrome Hearts clothing and jewelry with hair styled by celebrity hairstylist Oribe Canales, on April 9, 2010.

chapter 8

THE MAGIC OF BARBIE

Barbie has fans of all ages, races, and genders. They live all over the world, and their affection for Barbie is enduring. But can it last forever? The best answer comes from the children and parents, the fans and collectors who continue to be inspired, delighted, and empowered by Barbie. Here's a wonderful example from one mother and daughter:

Kara Norman's ten-year-old daughter, Kennedy, was excited to try the simple experiments in her new chemistry set. She had a great idea. Why not use the lab set to create a pretend lab/classroom with her "I Can Be . . . Teacher" Barbie doll? She used other Barbie dolls as students and was soon using her teacher Barbie to explain the experiments to her "class." Kennedy, wearing protective goggles and engrossed in her pretend job, wrote out her pH test results on a whiteboard.

Kara, who runs Empower Her, Inc., a nonprofit to empower women and girls, thinks it is important to get girls interested in STEM (science, technology, engineering, and math fields). Kara was delighted to see Kennedy take a science kit and turn it into an imaginary world, which gave her an idea.

At Kennedy's birthday party, Kara based her theme on Barbie's "I Can Be" line of career dolls. Kennedy's friends came dressed as what they wanted to be when they grew up. Kara said, "I didn't stop there. I had someone come in and do a robotics demonstration with the girls and boys, and at the end of the party they built their own robots."

The genius of Barbie has always been that she is what her fans make her. Absent the ingredient of human imagination, Barbie is just a doll. She is simply pieces of molded plastic in the shape of a woman.

OPPOSITE: Barbara Handler—daughter of Ruth and Elliot Handler, and namesake for the Barbie doll—poses with a Barbie doll after placing her hands in cement that will adorn the sidewalk at the Egyptian Theatre in Hollywood, California, in an event designed to honor Barbie on November 13, 2002.

But her creator, Ruth Handler, understood the depth of children's imaginations. She had seen it in her daughter, along with something more. She witnessed the deep desire of children to play and pretend about the world.

Barbie, with her ageless features, is timeless. To one four-year-old, she may be a dress-up doll, to another, a doll to act out her dreams. But to an adolescent, Barbie can take on different roles in different worlds, including those of fantasy. With her ever-changing fashions and, more recently, her broad selection of face sculpts, skin tones, body types, and hair choices, Barbie offers her fans infinite possibilities.

Barbie has helped out at lemonade stands, gone on vacation, and starred in countless home videos and photographs. Girls have imagined her in jobs well beyond those suggested by Mattel. She has also turned magical as a fairy, witch, and countless creatures known only to the children who make them up.

Barbie is not just for girls.

Stanley Colorite's smile is as bright as his pink suit jacket and matching shoes. He's the biggest Barbie collector in the United States, with more than ten thousand dolls. All his dolls are taken out of the boxes and put in air-sealed containers. He also collects Dreamhouses and cars.

His house in Florida is a joyous, colorful display of all things Barbie. Dolls line the walls in neat rows. As Stanley said, "It's nice to wake up every day and have beauty around you."

Stanley's interest was sparked by his mother, who was also a collector. He started out with Jem and the Holograms and G.I. Joe, but in 1992, tragedy struck. His mother died in a fire, and in memory of her, he kept her collection going. By 1997, he was a Barbie collector. "I went to the Salvation Army, and bought the 1992 Happy Holiday Barbie. She was my first." He also bought the dentist Barbie, which had jointed elbows and a button to push that made her talk. He liked that she could cross her legs, and that her wrists moved like Jem's. He liked to play with the dolls that sparked his sense of fun and his imagination.

Stanley's mother's dolls were naked, so he bought an identification book and started buying clothes that went with them. He also went to doll shows and spent hours in the Barbie aisle at Toys "R" Us. His mother had dolls from the 1970s that she bought at flea markets, and he managed to dress them all.

The oldest doll Stanley has is the Number Three Barbie. His collection goes from 1960 to the present. Stanley said, "I also have a massive Jem collection, but my main thing is Barbie. I also have every Midge, Teresa, PJ, Stacey, and Skipper."

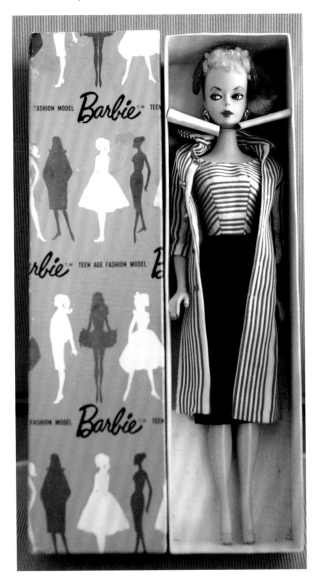

ABOVE: A vintage 1959 Barbie doll dressed in Roman Holiday attire is displayed during the 2006 Barbie Doll Collectors Convention, where hundreds of dealers and collectors buy, sell, and trade Barbie dolls and accessories, in Los Angeles, California, on July 26, 2006.

TOP: Kitturah Westenhouser, collector and author of *The Story of Barbie*, poses with part of her Barbie collection. **BOTTOM**: Kitty Stuart—owner of Kitty's Collectables, one of the largest vintage Barbie doll dealerships—poses in 1997 with an "artist doll" by David Escobedo that is sculpted in Kitty's likeness, next to some of her thousands of Barbie dolls. Kitty is wearing a "Barbie at the Beach" hand-painted jacket by popular designer Tony Alamo.

How does Stanley find new dolls for his collection? All sorts of ways. He shared one example from 2001. "FAO Schwarz went out of business in Michigan, where I'm from. I had a lady friend who was general manager of FAO. She sold the window displays of the Bob Mackie Barbies. I got them all for fifty dollars each, with the boxes that said 'FAO Schwarz exclusive.'"

He said, "Barbie would live on even if she was discontinued, because of secondary markets like eBay. There are so many Barbies out in the world. She'll always be around."

And last, but certainly not least, there's one collector who outshines them all.

Bettina Dorfmann lives in Dusseldorf, Germany, which straddles the Rhine River and is a city known for its fashion industry and art scene. For twenty-five years, Bettina—with her broad smile and long, straight, natural blonde hair— has amassed the largest-known collection of Barbie dolls in

TOP: Bettina Dorfmann, the owner of the world's largest Barbie collection, poses in front of some of her dolls. **BOTTOM LEFT**: Bettina Dorfmann poses with a vintage Number One Barbie from 1959. **TOP RIGHT**: Not just a collector, Bettina Dorfmann is also a doll doctor and runs a Barbie hospital from her home, where she repairs broken dolls sent to her from all over the world.

the world. *Guinness World Records 2011* recognized Bettina for owning fifteen thousand Barbie dolls. In 2023, she had 18,500 dolls and still held the record.

Bettina's interest began at six years old with a blonde-haired Midge. "I played with the doll every day with my friends. We could sew for the doll, and we could play all situations from our own life, from the television, or from other stories."

Bettina didn't start collecting until 1993. She tried to give her childhood dolls to her daughter, who wanted more modern dolls. Bettina realized that her dolls reminded her of her own childhood and her friends and birthdays and Christmas. She realized something important and thought, *Barbie is a mirror of our own life!* Naturally, the first doll in her collection was a rare 1963 Midge doll.

After some years of collecting, Bettina started to repair Barbie dolls. She created her own Barbie clinic, the only one in Germany. Then she began work on a Barbie museum and started holding Barbie exhibitions. Her collection really began to grow at that time, because her exhibitions required a lot of dolls. She became such an expert that she has been called on to create reports for legal cases or insurance claims that involve the doll.

Bettina told the *World Record Academy*, "There's probably nothing I don't know about Barbie. It drives my husband crazy every time I come home with a new doll. When I tell him it's getting harder and harder to get the rare ones he laughs and said, 'That's because they are all here in the house!'"

Bettina said, "Everything about her—her clothes, hairstyles, makeup, sports, jobs, designer items, Hollywood glamour—are all things from our lives. And she is always up to date, including accessories, which are very important, and her jobs, like going from stewardess to pilot."

In the end, Bettina summed it up for everyone who has ever loved a Barbie doll, "Barbie is a mirror of our world. She is forever."

FOLLOWING: Barbie doll collector Tina Brettnacher presents some of her rarest and oldest dolls to celebrate Barbie's 60th birthday during an exhibition dedicated to Barbie at *La Nef des Jouets* in Soultz, France, which ran from March 9, to June 30, 2019.

Barbie et Ken en tenue de mariés
1963

chapter 9

BARBIE MAKES HISTORY

I n 2023, the *Barbie* movie, staring Margot Robbie and Ryan Gosling, smashed records for Warner Bros. Studios' biggest releases, such as *Harry Potter and the Deathly Hallows Part 2* and *Batman: The Dark Night*. The July 21st date marked the biggest opening weekend for a film directed by a woman, Greta Gerwig. Gerwig now also holds the prize for highest-grossing film directed by a woman.

As the box office numbers were tallied, more records were broken: Highest opening for a non-sequel, biggest opening for a toy-based film, biggest opening for a movie without IMAX (though the IMAX version later opened), impressive of all: the *Barbie* movie passed a billion dollars in worldwide ticket sales in less than a month.

Written by Gerwig and Noah Baumbach, the *Barbie* movie showed the world that female directors with female lead actors can carry box office sales. And not just that, the movie has proven Barbie is more popular now than she has ever been.

The 2023 *Barbie* movie was not Barbie's first foray into film. Over 40 feature-length animated films have been released since 2001. *Barbie in the Nutcracker* was the first in a long list of reimagined stories and fairytales that became so popular, they paved the way for original Barbie screenplays and sequels.

By 2017, Barbie had her own television shows, including the global sensation, *Barbie Dreamhouse Adventures*. Her place in the entertainment marketplace was well-established. So why was *Barbie*, the live action movie, the one to break all records?

OPPOSITE: Greta Gerwig, Ynon Kreiz, Margot Robbie. 2023.

Many reporters and scholars have tried to answer this question. There's no one answer, but rather it seems that a wholly original film, plus timing, marketing, and Barbie's iconic status, all contributed to create more than a movie, but a historic, cultural event.

According to Maria Theresa Hart, who has written extensively about the Barbie brand, part of the movie's charm is nostalgia. In a July 24, 2023, interview in *Vox Magazine,* she said, "I mean, it's this moment where you recognize that you are not alone – there's so many other people that are just desperate to get back into their toy boxes and want to relive their moments they had in their childhood bedroom."

In *American Magazine,* writers Brigid McCabe and Laura Oldfeather attributed the popularity to the film's attentiveness to the current social climate. "Through on-the-nose commentary on everything from Barbie's representation of independent female adulthood to her unrealistic, idealized body proportions, Gerwig makes a movie as layered and paradoxical as the reputation of the doll itself."

Even *Psychology Today* stepped into analysis. "The problem is that Barbie's life is perfect, but our lives are far from perfect. How and why would we then relate to Barbie's ideal life?" Bence Nanay, Ph.D., then goes on to suggest that Barbie's decision of whether to stay comfortably in Barbie Land or challenge herself in the real world is similar to the choices that the viewers face every day as well.

On *MovieWeb,* Olly Dyche summarized the film's popularity. "With Greta Gerwig tackling the world and lore of *Barbie* and incorporating almost every Barbie ever made, the award-winning director has created an impressively diverse cast and flick. Including gender, race, size, sexuality, and culture, *Barbie* is a film that will speak to and connect to everyone and anyone, and for a movie as large and successful as *Barbie,* that's a deeply admirable achievement."

There may never be consensus as to why this movie drew the entire world's attention at this precise moment, but one thing is certain: the film stayed true to Ruth Handler's philosophy that "through this doll, girls could be anything they wanted to be." This importantly resonated with audiences from all backgrounds and lifestyles.

Actor Margot Robbie looks the role of a "Stereotypical Barbie doll" in the film. Chairman and Chief Executive Officer of Mattel Ynon Kreiz spoke about the casting choice to *The New York Times* in 2023. He said, "Our vision for Barbie was someone with a strong voice, a clear message, with cultural resonance that would make a societal impact."

Since the doll's inception, Mattel has held to the vision that all girls should be able see themselves in Barbie. Christie, Barbie doll's first Black friend, was released in 1968. In 1980, Black and Hispanic dolls named "Barbie" themselves were released. These dolls were no longer Barbie doll's friends but shared the iconic name. Mattel has made inclusion and diversity a core goal for the entire line.

There are currently 175 different Barbie dolls. Mattel's website boasts 35 skin tones, 97 hair styles, and 9 body types. Those numbers are growing each year.

Barbie represents *everyone.* Barbie doll has *Down syndrome.* She is in a wheelchair. She has a prosthetic leg. Barbie doll takes on jobs that are underrepresented by women, like paleontologists and the U.S. President.

As Josh Bullmore, Chief Strategy Officer, Leo Burnett London, said, "This is a Barbie-themed example of the broader truth that everyone wins from inclusivity."

The *Barbie* movie's opening scene highlights this substantive change, where Robbie's iconic Barbie greets her friends and neighbors by saying, "Hi, Barbie!" and they all return the greeting.

Coming off this success, Mattel is now much more than the toy manufacturer that was founded in a garage— it is an intellectual property-driven toy company managing IP franchises.

Film, television, consumer products, digital experiences. Mattel is now in every aspect of entertainment, giving the company the experience and expertise to take the popularity of the *Barbie* movie into new realms.

There were more than 165 consumer product partnerships for the *Barbie* movie. Barbie is reaching

OPPOSITE: Margot Robbie poses as Barbie in the original bathing suit from Barbie's 1959 launch.

millions, even billions, of buyers, collectors, and fans through these partnerships. Since the film's opening in 2023, the whole world is rapidly turning pink.

Several exciting ventures are on the horizon. Mattel Adventure Park is opening in Arizona in 2024 with a Barbie Beach House. New Barbie dolls and animated shows for television are also heading to market.

With the *Barbie* movie as a template, Mattel has announced 14 other live-action motion pictures in development with major studios, including a Lena Dunham directed Polly Pocket film starring and co-produced by Lily Collins, and a Hot Wheels story produced by J.J. Abrams' Bad Robot to be distributed by Warner Bros. Pictures.

The true legacy of Barbie can be seen in her creator, Ruth Handler. Ruth fought against the status quo, had an instinct for marketing, and showed determination to achieve her dreams. Her dedication to bring Barbie doll to market was challenged again and again. But Ruth refused to let her dream go. From the moment she saw her daughter, Barbara, playing with paper dolls, Ruth knew that she could create something special, something that didn't exist, and most importantly, something that would inspire imaginative play. To get the doll made, she had to push past Mattel's early designers and engineers. Ruth searched for resources and hired helpers who shared her vision. Her doll was going to be glamorous and allow for the most creative play, as well as inspire lofty personal goals.

Marketing to television was new, but Ruth knew this was the only way to get Barbie doll the attention she deserved. The debut toy fair failed, but children responded to the marketing on television and all those who had told Ruth "No" soon learned that they were wrong. Barbie doll went on to be a blockbuster toy.

And years later, the *Barbie* movie became a blockbuster film.

Ruth Handler was also a breast cancer survivor, which inspired her second passion project. Ruth's "Nearly Me" products for Breast Cancer survivors also went on to great success. She sold that company to Kimberly-Clark in the 1990s.

ABOVE: Mattel officially partnered with Spirit Halloween stores to produce the rollerskating costume seen in the live-action movie and inspired by the 1994 "Hot Skatin' Barbie."

ABOVE: Official Mattel collaborations (clockwise from top left) with Impala Skates, BÉIS, and Wrangler Jeans.

ABOVE: Mattel understands the power of representation. New dolls, released each year, reflect and inspire the next generation.

Today, Ruth's dedication continues in the form of The Ruth Handler Mentorship Program for Women in Toys. This program provides opportunities for a new generation of leaders.

In the *Barbie* movie, Ruth Handler is played by Rhea Pearlman. Barbie, in the midst of an existential identity crisis, accidentally enters a dream-space where she touches the hand of her creator Ruth and asks for help in becoming human. Ruth replies, "You don't need my permission . . . I can't control you any more than I could control my own daughter. I named you after her: Barbara. And I always hoped for you, like I hoped for her. We mothers stand still so our daughters can look back to see how far they've come."

LEFT: Amputee Barbie helps children relate to their own experiences. **RIGHT**: Ruth Handler with her Nearly Me Prosthetics.

FIRST CAREERS

In the early '60s, to inspire girls and support more women entering the workforce, Barbie released her first careers: Fashion Editor (1960), Registered Nurse (1961), Flight Attendant (1961), and Executive Career Girl (1963).

RUTH HANDLER

Barbie creator Ruth Handler saw her daughter's toy choices were limited. She could only play out being a mom or caregiver, whereas her son had toys that allowed him to imagine himself as a firefighter, astronaut, doctor, and more. This inspired Ruth to create a doll that showed girls they had choices— that they could be anything.

FIRST DREAMHOUSE

Before women were even allowed to open their own bank accounts, Barbie bought her first Dreamhouse in 1962. Barbie represented women in new ways, becoming a symbol of independence and empowerment. With its mid-century modern décor, hi-fi stereo, and slimline furniture, girls could imagine entertaining friends or relaxing in a stylish living room.

KEN DEBUTS

After receiving hundreds of letters from little girls asking for a boyfriend for Barbie, Mattel debuted Ken on March 11, 1961. He came dressed in red swimming trunks, with a yellow towel and sandals.

1959   1960   1961   1962

BARBIE DEBUTS

On March 9, 1959, Barbie debuted at the American Toy Fair in New York. The first Barbie wore a black-and-white striped swimsuit and her signature ponytail. Toy buyers were skeptical because Barbie was unlike the baby and toddler dolls that were popular at the time. They doubted she would be successful, but Barbie took the world by storm, letting girls imagine their futures like never before from that moment on.

FIRST CAR

In 1962, Barbie hit the road in her first car—an Austin-Healey 3000 MKII BN7. The sporty, peach, two-seater convertible was perfect for Barbie to zip around in, and it set the stage for girls to image what the life of a woman could be.

FIRST COMMERCIAL

Barbie appeared in her first commercial, airing on ABC during the *Mickey Mouse Club* program in 1959. The TV commercial spoke directly to kids and presented Barbie as if she were a real person. After the spot aired, Barbie dolls flew off the shelves, selling 350,000 the first year.

BARBIE FAN CLUB

When excited kids starting contacting Mattel to share their love of Barbie, they decided to create a fan club. Barbie Fan Club members received a letter, membership card, and a subscription to the *Barbie Magazine*. Girls were also sent materials to help them start their own local fan club chapters.

MALIBU BARBIE

In 1971, Malibu Barbie debuted with a new face sculpt and eyes that faced forward—instead of glancing to the side—for the first time. She was suntanned with long straight hair, and solidified Barbie as a quintessential sun-loving, California girl.

BARBIE INTRODUCES CHRISTIE

In support of Equal Rights, Barbie released Christie, one of the first Black dolls. Christie was created as a friend of Barbie and came dressed in a mod-inspired swimsuit with a short '60s hairstyle.

SURGEON BARBIE

The first time Barbie put on scrubs was in 1973, when very few women were in the operating room. With her surgical mask and mini stethoscope, Surgeon Barbie let girls play out their dreams of treating patients and saving lives.

| 1965 | 1967 | 1968 | 1971 | 1973 | 1975 |

ASTRONAUT BARBIE

In 1965, Barbie went galactic four years before man landed on the moon. Miss Astronaut Barbie celebrated the excitement of the space program and exploring new frontiers. Dressed in a cool space suit and helmet, she showed girls they could reach for the stars.

FIRST CELEBRITY DOLL

The first celebrity Barbie doll was based on the British fashion model Twiggy. The original Twiggy doll had iconic Twiggy makeup and wore a yellow, green, and blue vertical-striped mini dress and yellow boots. She was the beginning of a long line of dolls made to resemble celebrities and fashion's elite.

FIRST CAMPER

In 1971, Barbie was ready to go on adventures in her first camper. Girls could imagine exploring the great outdoors in a groovy camper with a picnic setup, pop-out tent, and sleeping bags.

GOLD MEDAL BARBIE

In 1975, Barbie competed for her home country. Barbie came dressed in a patriotic red, white, and blue uniform with a gold medal around her neck so girls could fulfill their ambition to win big. The Barbie team also included an ice skater, a ski jumper, and a track and field runner.

CEO BARBIE

In 1985, Day-to-Night Barbie broke the glass ceiling as a CEO. Day-to-Night Barbie could go from running the boardroom in her pink power suit to a fun night out on the town. She celebrated the workplace evolution of the era and showed girls they could have it all.

FIRST DIVERSE DOLLS NAMED BARBIE

Over the years, many diverse dolls were available, but they were always friends of Barbie. In 1980, Mattel released the first Black and Hispanic dolls named Barbie.

HEADLINE: DOLLS OF THE WORLD

In 1981, Barbie released its Dolls of the World collection. Each doll wore an ensemble inspired by its country's traditional customs and fashions. The collection celebrated different cultures and traditions while introducing girls to the world through play.

"WE GIRLS CAN DO ANYTHING" CAMPAIGN

In 1985, Barbie launched the We Girls Can Do Anything ad campaign. The series of ads encouraged girls to believe in themselves and their dreams. The commercial featured a song that had girls singing, "We girls can do anything, right Barbie?" and "Anything is possible as long as I try."

1980   **1981**   **1984**   **1985**

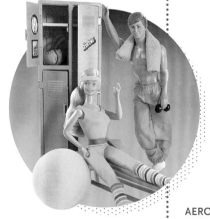

FIRST BARBIE CONVENTION

The Barbie Collector Convention—which brings thousands of Barbie fans together each year—started in October 1980 when 100 collectors gathered in New York City. The first national gathering marked the beginning of enthusiasts from all over the world getting together to celebrate their love of Barbie.

AEROBICS INSTRUCTOR BARBIE

Aerobics Instructor Barbie embraced the fun workout trend of the '80s, wearing a turquoise leotard, headband, and striped legwarmers. The posable doll could even dance and high kick! The doll was later featured in the 1999 animated Pixar film, *Toy Story 2*.

FIRST FASHION PARTNERSHIP

Barbie has worked with more fashion designers than any other brand in the world. Her first fashion partnership was in 1985, when Oscar de la Renta created a line of designer clothes for Barbie. The glamorous jewel tone and metallic outfits brought runway fun to young fashion lovers, sparking their imaginations and creativity. This was the start of many fashion collaborations to come.

BARBIE AND THE ROCKERS

In 1986, Barbie took to the stage as lead singer of her New Wave rock group, Barbie and the Rockers. The characters Dee Dee, Dana, Diva, and Derek were introduced as her bandmates. These dazzling superstars were ready to rock with their bright instruments and '80s attire.

PILOT BARBIE

In 1989, Barbie prepared for take-off at a time when very few women were in the pilot seat. Barbie soared to new elevations in her pink pilot outfit, showing girls the sky's the limit when you're free to believe.

BARBIE RUNS FOR PRESIDENT

Barbie has been running for president in every election year since 1992. The first President Barbie came with an American-themed dress for an inaugural ball and a red suit for her duties in the Oval Office. In 2016, Barbie released an all-female ticket with a president and vice president doll set to inspire girls to believe they can be anything—including leader of the free world.

1986   1989   1992   1993

ANDY WARHOL PAINTING

Andy Warhol made his mark by creating images of American icons. Barbie was added to the list when Warhol painted her in 1986. The first Barbie portrait was reportedly inspired by Warhol's muse, BillyBoy*, a jewelry designer and member of New York's downtown scene in the 1980s, who owned a vast collection of Barbie dolls.

HEADLINE ARMY OFFICER BARBIE

Barbie has served her country many times, starting in 1989 as Army Officer Barbie. She has represented every branch of the military, letting girls play out missions by land, sea, and sky.

TOTALLY HAIR BARBIE

Totally Hair Barbie is the best-selling Barbie doll to date. She celebrated the loud fashions and big hair craze of the early '90s and featured the longest hair ever on a Barbie doll. To celebrate the doll's 25th anniversary, she was re-released in 2017.

POLICE OFFICER BARBIE

Pink may be her favorite color, but in 1993, Barbie proudly wore blue. When very few women were police officers, Barbie showed girls they could join the force.

SIGN LANGUAGE BARBIE

In 2001, Sign Language Teacher Barbie empowered girls to learn new languages. Her hand was molded into the ASL sign for "I love you," and she came with illustrations of common words in sign language and fingerspelling for each letter of the alphabet.

PALEONTOLOGIST BARBIE

In 1997, Paleontologist Barbie inspired girls to discover new things—like hidden fossils! With her cool dinosaur-themed outfit and accessories, Paleontologist Barbie was ready to dig up some fun.

FIRST FEATURE-LENGTH FILM

In 2001, Barbie starred in her first feature-length film, Barbie™ in *The Nutcracker*, on CBS. The movie tells the tale of Clara and her amazing nutcracker, who set off on an adventure to find the Sugarplum Princess. Barbie shows girls that if you are kind, clever, and brave, anything is possible.

WINTER SPORTS BARBIE

In 1995, Barbie encouraged girls to explore a range of winter sports including snowboarding, which was predominately an all-male sport at the time. With Winter Sports Barbie, girls could imagine hitting the slopes and carving up some fresh powder.

| 1995 | 1997 | 2000 | 2001 | 2002 |

AVIATOR BARBIE

In 2002, Aviator Barbie took girls' imaginations to new heights. Dressed in a cool flight suit and helmet, she was ready for any mission or rescue effort. She inspired future aviators to play out their dreams of soaring through the sky.

EXTREME 360° BARBIE

In 2000, Extreme 360° Barbie inspired girls to go big. She came with a skateboard, rollerblades, and had bendable limbs so she could do awesome tricks.

FIREFIGHTER BARBIE

In 1995, Firefighter Barbie showed girls they could be everyday heroes. With her yellow firefighter uniform and helmet, girls could imagine putting out fires and saving the day.

COMPUTER ENGINEER BARBIE

In 2010, Barbie launched its Career of the Year program. For the first time in the brand's history, the public was invited to vote for the 126th Barbie career. Female engineers rallied to vote for Computer Engineer Barbie, hoping to bring more recognition to women in computer professions.

ZOOLOGIST BARBIE

Barbie, the ultimate animal lover, has had many different careers taking care of them. In 2006, Zoologist Barbie let girls explore their dreams of helping and nurturing wildlife.

RACE CAR DRIVER BARBIE

In 2010, Barbie took on several more underrepresented careers including race car driver. Race Car Driver Barbie encouraged girls to rev up their dreams of going fast and winning the race.

| 2006 | 2009 | 2010 | 2011 |

NEWS ANCHOR BARBIE

In 2010, with women still underrepresented in the newsroom, Barbie was reporting live—showing girls they have a place in front of or behind the camera.

ARCHITECT BARBIE

In 2011, Architect Barbie was ready to design new spaces with her hard hat, blueprints, and Dreamhouse model. Architect Barbie let girls dream about constructing worlds built by their imaginations.

FIRST NY RUNWAY SHOW

In 2009, Barbie held her first New York runway show at Mercedes-Benz Fashion Week to celebrate her 50th anniversary. Fifty of the world's top designers created haute couture looks inspired by Barbie and her iconic history.

FIRST APP

In 2010, Barbie launched its first app, Barbie Fashionistas Swappin' Styles. The app let users style Barbie and create their own fashion looks.

BARBIE VLOGGER

In 2015, Barbie launched a vlog on YouTube to talk directly to girls about issues they face. The animated series features Barbie discussing a range of topics including depression, bullying, the health benefits of meditation, and how girls have a habit of apologizing when they don't have anything to be sorry about.

BARBIE INTRODUCES NEW BODY TYPES

In 2016, to better reflect the world that girls see today, Barbie introduced three new body types: curvy, petite, and tall. The launch of the new body types landed Barbie on the cover of *Time* magazine.

DETECTIVE BARBIE

In 2014, Detective Barbie hit the mean streets of Malibu with her badge and walkie-talkie to solve the city's mysteries and inspire girls to go on crime-fighting adventures.

FILM DIRECTOR BARBIE

In 2015, when female directors were still underrepresented in the movie industry, Barbie took on Hollywood. Film Director Barbie inspired girls to explore the exciting world of making movies and let them play out their dreams of being on set.

BARBIE IN THE CULINARY ARTS

In 2016, with female head chefs still underrepresented, Barbie inspired girls to cook up some fun. With Barbie as a head chef or pastry chef, young foodies could imagine whipping up gourmet meals and classy desserts.

2014　　　2015　　　2016

@BARBIESTYLE

In 2014, Barbie became a social media influencer with the launch of the @barbiestyle Instagram account. The account was created to celebrate pop culture moments through the eyes of an icon and quickly became a leading fashion influencer channel. From fashion and art, to culture and travel, @barbiestyle excites followers as only Barbie can.

BARBIE SHEROES

In 2015, Barbie celebrated female heroes who inspire girls by breaking boundaries and expanding the possibilities for women everywhere. One-of-a-kind dolls were created for each of the Shero honorees, including Ava DuVernay, Emmy Rossum, Eva Chen, Kristin Chenoweth, Sydney "Mayhem" Keiser, and Trisha Yearwood.

MARTIAL ARTIST BARBIE

Through the years, Barbie has represented a wide range of sports. In 2016, Martial Artist Barbie was added to list. Barbie was ready to spar with her black belt, trophy, and breakable wooden board. She inspired young athletes to explore the exciting world of martial arts.

BARBIE LOUVRE EXHIBIT

In 2016, the Musée des Arts Décoratifs at the Louvre, in Paris, held an exhibition dedicated to Barbie. The exhibit featured over 700 dolls and showed how Barbie has evolved with society since 1959.

BUILDER BARBIE

In 2017, Builder Barbie introduced girls to the world of construction and inspired them to build big dreams. With her hardhat, toolbelt, and building blocks, Barbie was ready to create worlds where anything is possible.

BARBIE DREAMHOUSE ADVENTURES

In 2018, the animated series *Barbie Dreamhouse Adventures* was released on Netflix. The hilarious and heartwarming series let fans peek into the everyday life of Barbie as she embarked on exciting adventures with her family, friends, and Ken!

60TH ANNIVERSARY

To mark this milestone, the brand hosted events around the world, launched the Barbie Dream Gap Project Fund, introduced a commemorative doll collection, and more.

#MOREROLEMODELS

Barbie shone a light on empowering role models from the past and present in an effort to inspire more girls. The campaign, #MoreRoleModels, honored extraordinary women from around the world on International Women's Day. The Inspiring Women doll line also launched and featured Frida Kahlo, Katherine Johnson, and Amelia Earhart.

2017 — 2018 — 2019

BEEKEEPER BARBIE

In 2018, Beekeeper Barbie was released to teach the next generation about the importance of bees and how to care for them. Equipped with her beekeeping suit, Barbie was ready to raise her hive and harvest honey.

DREAM GAP PROJECT

Barbie launched the Dream Gap Project, an ongoing global initiative that gives girls the resources and support they need to continue to believe they can be anything. The initiative includes funding research, highlighting positive role models, and producing content and products that inspire girls.

THE NEW CREW

In 2017, the Barbie Fashionistas crew became more diverse than ever before, featuring more skin tones, eye colors, hairstyles, and fashions. Ken also got an update, with two more body types added to the lineup: broad and slim. #NextGenKen had a variety of new looks including a man bun, cornrows, and freckles.

BARBIE + TYNKER

In 2018, Barbie encouraged girls to explore STEM through imaginative play and a partnership with Tynker, the award-winning computing platform. With the Robotics Engineer Barbie doll and You Can Be Anything programming lessons, girls learned about coding while discovering new careers.

A NEW BARBIE IN TOWN

Mattel introduced a prominent Black lead—Barbie "Brooklyn" Roberts—in content, toy, and publishing to ensure girls see themselves as lead characters.

THANK YOU, HEROES

To honor the everyday heroes who stepped up during the COVID-19 pandemic, Mattel created a new line of dolls that included medical professionals, food-service workers, and firefighters. During a week in May, Mattel donated a doll to the First Responders Children's Foundation for every doll sold.

HAPPY ANNIVERSARY KEN

Marking Ken's debut in 1961, the sixtieth anniversary celebration doll was released under the trademarked Gold Label. Designer Bill Greening maintained Ken's classic beach style with a "Genuine Ken" wrist tag.

2020

2021

BARBIE CONFRONTS RACISM

In an episode of the Barbie web show, "Barbie Vlogs," Barbie talked with her friend Nikki about her experiences with racism. The pair also covered white privilege, racial bias, and what it means to be a true ally.

NEW DIVERSE SHERO DOLLS

The 2020 Shero line included Paralympic champion Madison de Rozario, who was awed by the accuracy of the details including the reduced race chair measurements.

THE FUTURE OF PINK IS GREEN

In June, Barbie launched a campaign designed to support recycling and ocean advocacy. Mattel announced their goal to achieve 95% recycled or FSC-certified paper and wood fiber materials used in Barbie packaging by the end of 2021. Three new dolls and the beach shack were made from recycled plastics.

Barbie is everything.

MATTEL ADVENTURE PARK

A new theme park is set to open near Phoenix. Arizona and will include a Barbie Beach House, along with other rides based on Mattel toys and properties. Visitors to the Beach House will find themselves in a Barbie Dream Closet and can play along through state of the art interactive technology.

BARBIE: THE MOVIE

July 21, 2023 the first live-action Barbie movie was released, smashing box office records and creating hundreds of new licensing deals.

2022   2023   2024

BARBIE: MERMAID POWER

The 40th musical adventure Barbie film starred Barbie "Malibu" Roberts, Barbie "Brooklyn" Roberts, Skipper, Stacie, and Chelsea. The girls transformed into mermaids to help their friend under the sea.

BARBIE: THE ALBUM

The film soundtrack featured music by Billie Eilish, Dua Lipa, Nicki Minaj & Ice Spice, and Sam Smith. The album received several Grammy nominations including Record of the Year.

COMING SOON

Launching new Barbies with disability representation remains a core focus for Mattel. New inclusive dolls will continue to give girls a broad range of play opportunities.

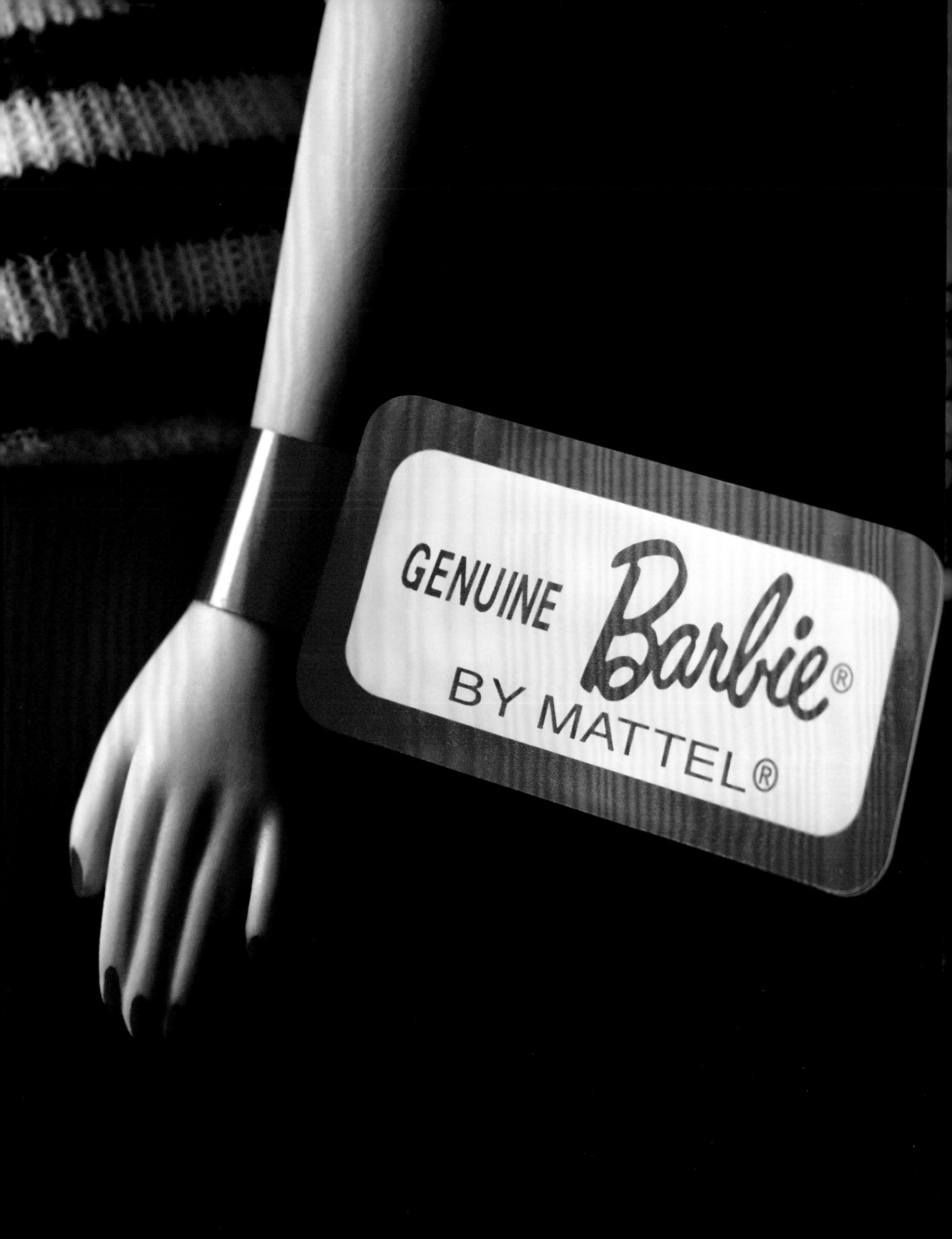
GENUINE Barbie®
BY MATTEL®

BIBLIOGRAPHY

Many of the following books and articles were useful in writing this book, and serve as a resource guide for anyone interested in Barbie.

Abrams, Rachel. "Barbie Adds Curvy and Tall to Body Shapes." *New York Times.* January 28, 2016. https://www.nytimes.com/2016/01/29/business/barbie-now-in-more-shapes.html

Abrams, Rachel. "Mattel Aims to Reanimate Sales with Talking Barbie." *New York Times.* October 15, 2015. https://www.nytimes.com/2015/10/16/business/mattel-aims-to-reanimate-sales-with-interactive-barbie.html

Abrams, Rachel. "Mattel Takes a Risk, with Barbie and Bugs." *New York Times.* December 28, 2015. https://www.nytimes.com/2015/12/28/business/mattel-takes-a-risk-with-barbie-and-bugs.html

Alexander, Hilary. "Barbie celebrates 50th birthday with her very own fashion show." *The Telegraph.* February 14, 2009.

Augustyniak, J. Michael. *The Barbie Doll Boom: Identification and Values.* Collector Books, 1996.

Augustyniak, J. Michael. *Barbie Doll Around the World 1964–2007:* Identification & Values. Collector Books, 2007.

Augustyniak, J. Michael. *Barbie Doll Photo Album 1959 to 2009.* Collector Books, 2010.

Augustyniak, J. Michael. *Collector's Encyclopedia of Barbie Doll Collector's Editions.* Collector Books, 2007.

Bansal, Avnie. "Barbie Does Diversity: A Cultural Step-Change, or Just a Brand Playing Catch-up with Its Consumers?" *Creative Salon,* 2023, creative.salon/articles/features/this-barbie-is-inclusive.

"Barbie Diversity: Mattel." *Mattel Shop,* 2023, shop.mattel.com/pages/barbie-diversity.

Barbielist Holland. "1959–2014 Fifty-five Years Big Changes of the Barbie Doll (Part I)." BarbielistHolland.wordpress.com (blog). October 18, 2014. https://barbielistholland.wordpress.com/2014/10/18/1959-2014-fityfive-years-big-changes-of-the-barbie-doll-part-i/.

Barrowclough, Anne. "Rolf Hausser: Creator of the Bild Lilli Doll." FondationTanagra.com. n.d. http://www.fondationtanagra.com/en/article/rolf-hausser-the-creator-of-the-bild-lilli-doll/page/lilli-in-america.

BillyBoy*. *Barbie: Her Life and Times.* Three Rivers Press. 1992.

Blitman, Joe. *Barbie and Her Mod, Mod, Mod, Mod, World of Fashion.* Hobby House Press, 1996.

Blitman, Joe. *Francie & Her Mod, Mod, Mod World of Fashion.* Hobby House Press, 1996.

Cain Miller, Claire. "Barbie's New Job, Computer Engineer." *New York Times.* February 15, 2010.

https://archive.nytimes.com/query.nytimes.com/gst/fullpage-9D03E3DD113DF936A25751C0A9669D8B63.html.

Carberry, James. "Valley of the Dolls." *Wall Street Journal.* June 20, 1973.

Carvajal, Doreen. "With Museum Shows in Europe, Barbie Gets Her Moment with the Masters." *New York Times.* March 11, 2016. https://www.nytimes.com/2016/03/11/arts/design/with-museum-shows-in-europe-barbie-gets-her-moment-with-the-masters.html

Clement, Douglas P. "The Female Identity, Discussed in Art." *New York Times.* April 3, 2016, https://www.nytimes.com/2016/04/03/nyregion/the-female-identity-discussed-in-art.html

Clifford, Stephanie. "More Dads Buy the Toys, So Barbie, and Stores, Get Makeovers." *New York Times.* December 4, 2012. https://www.nytimes.com/2012/12/04/business/more-dads-buy-the-toys-so-barbie-and-stores-get-makeovers.html

Creswell, Julie. "Mattel's Revival Plan: Bet on Barbie, the Movie." *New York Times.* December 13, 2018. https://www.nytimes.com/2018/12/13/business/mattel-barbie-movie-ynon-kreiz.html

D'Amato, Jennie. *Barbie: All Dolled Up: Celebrating 50 Years of Barbie.* Running Press, 2009.

Deutsch, Stefanie. Barbie: *The First 30 Years 1959 Through 1989: An Identification and Value Guide.* Collector Books, 1995.

Dockterman, Eliana. "Barbie's Got a New Body." *Time Magazine.* January 28, 2016.

Dockterman, Eliana. "Inside the Barbie Movie: How the Massive Movie Came to Be." *Time,* 27 June 2023, time.com/6289864/barbie-time-cover-story/.

Dockterman, Eliana. "What to Know about Ruth Handler, the Creator of Barbie." *Time,* 21 July 2023, time.com/6293762/barbie-movie-ruth-handler/.

Dyche, Olly. "Why Barbie Is One of the Most Important and Progressive Movies of All Time." *MovieWeb,* 5 Aug. 2023, movieweb.com/why-barbie-is-one-of-the-most-important-and-progressive-movies/.

Eagan, Cindy. *The Story of Barbie and the Woman Who Created Her.* Random House, 2017.

Elliott, Stuart. "Barbie's Sports Illustrated Swimsuit Issue Causes a Stir Online." *New York Times,* February 2, 2014, https://www.nytimes.com/2014/02/12/business/media/barbies-sports-illustrated-swimsuit-issue-causes-a-stir-online.html

Elliott, Stuart. "Leaving Behind Malibu in Search of a New Dream Home." *New York Times.* February 7, 2013, https://www.nytimes.com/2013/02/07/business/media/barbie-to-sell-her-malibu-dreamhouse.html

Fennick, Janine. *The Collectible Barbie Doll: An Illustrated Guide to Her Dreamy World.* Courage Books, 1996.

Fennick, Janine. *Identifying Barbie Dolls: The New Compact Study Guide and Identifier.* Hachette, 1998.

Friedman, Vanessa. "Ken's New Look(s), Deconstructed." *New York Times.* June 21, 2017. https://www.nytimes.com/2017/06/21/fashion/mattel-barbie-ken-dolls.html

Fury, Alexander. "In Paris, the Shoe Designer Who Collects Dolls." *New York Times.* October 5, 2016. https://www.nytimes.com/2016/10/05/t-magazine/fashion/fabrizio-viti-dolls-louis-vuitton-shoes-fashion-week.html

Gerber, Robin. *Barbie and Ruth: The Story of the World's Most Famous Doll and the Woman Who Created Her.* HarperCollins, 2008.

Glassener, Abby. "Barbie Beginnings." *Sew News.* February-March, 2018.

Handler, Ruth. *Dream Doll: The Ruth Handler Story.* Longmeadow Press, 1995.

Hauser, Christine. "New Barbie Is Modeled After American Olympian Who Wears a Hijab." *New York Times.* November 14, 2017. https://www.nytimes.com/2017/11/14/business/barbie-hijab-ibtihaj-muhammad.html

Hazelhurst, Beatrice. "Tally of the Dolls." *New York Times.* October 30, 2018. https://www.nytimes.com/2018/10/30/style/instagram-dolls.html

Holder, Sandi. *Barbie: A Rare Beauty.* Krause Publications, 2010.

Hsu, Tiffany. "Mattel to Compete with Lego with $460 Million Mega Acquisition." *Los Angeles Times,* 28 Feb. 2014, www.latimes.com/business/la-fi-mo-mattel-lego-mega-20140228-story.html.

Itzkoff, Dave. "Barbie Heading to the Silver Screen." *New York Times.* September 25, 2009. https://archive.nytimes.com/query.nytimes.com/gst/fullpage-9C03E7D8153BF936A1575AC0A96F9C8B63.html.

James Shilkitus, Hillary. *The Complete & Unauthorized Guide to Vintage Barbie® Dolls: With Barbie®, Ken®, Francie®, Skipper® Fashions and the Whole Family.* Third edition. Schiffer, 2016.

James Shilkitus, Hillary. *It's All About the Accessories for the World's Most Fashionable Dolls, 1959–1972.* Third edition. Schiffer, 2016.

Kennedy, Randy. "Barbie, the Klimt Edition." *New York Times.* June 29, 2011. https://artsbeat.blogs.nytimes.com/2011/06/29/barbie-as-a-gustav-klimt-model.

Korbeck, Sharon. *The Best of Barbie: Four Decades of America's Favorite Doll.* Krause Publications, 2001.

Krier, Beth Ann. "Sweet 16: You've Come a Long Way, Barbie." *Los Angeles Times.* September 8, 1974.

Kushner, India. "The 'Barbie' Quote Rhea Perlman Delivers in the Movie Made Me Reexamine My Relationship with My Mom." *Yahoo! News*, Yahoo!, 9 Aug. 2023, news.yahoo.com/barbie-mother-quote-rhea-perlman-161804875.html#:~:text=Barbie%20meets%20her%20creator%2C%20Ruth,named%20you%20after%20her%3A%20Barbara.

Lambert, Molly. "Trixie Mattel Says Drag Queens Are Like Swiss Army Knives." *New York Times*. August 29, 2018. https://www.nytimes.com/2018/08/29/magazine/trixie-mattel-says-drag-queens-are-like-swiss-army-knives.html

Lord, M.G. *Forever Barbie: The Unauthorized Biography of a Real Doll*. Walker Books, 2004.

Lyons, Margaret. "How Much Watching Time Do You Have This Weekend?" *New York Times*. April 26, 2018. https://www.nytimes.com/2018/04/26/watching/what-to-watch-this-weekend-tv.html

MacArthur, Greg. "14 Upcoming Movies Based on Mattel Toys Releasing after Barbie." *ScreenRant*, 6 July 2023, screenrant.com/upcoming-movies-based-on-mattel-toys/#uno.

Mallenbaum, Carly. "Barbie in 2018 and beyond: How the doll is getting more inclusive." *USA Today*. April 25, 2018

Martin, Judith. "Interview with a Superstar." *The Washington Post*. April 7, 1974

Masters, Kim. "Pretty, Plastic Barbie: Forever What We Make her." National Public Radio (NPR). March 9, 2008. https://www.npr.org/templates/story/story.php?storyId=87997519.

Mattel Inc. "Mattel Bolsters Digital and Smart Technology Capabilities with Pair of Strategic Acquisitions." *PR Newswire: Press Release Distribution, Targeting, Monitoring and Marketing*, 29 June 2018, www.prnewswire.com/news-releases/mattel-bolsters-digital-and-smart-technology-capabilities-with-pair-of-strategic-acquisitions-300212408.html.

"Mattel." *Wikipedia*, Wikimedia Foundation, 7 Nov. 2023, en.wikipedia.org/wiki/Mattel#:~:text=The%20company%20purchased%20Fisher%2DPrice,prized%20property%2C%20Polly%20Pocket).

Melillo, Marcie. *The Ultimate Barbie Doll Book*. Krause Publications, 1996.

"Mentorship: Wit." *WiT Connects*, 2023, www.womenintoys.com/mentorship.

Montagne, Renee. "Bon Jour, Barbie! An American Icon Packs her Heels and Heads to France." National Public Radio (NPR). August 25, 2016. https://www.npr.org/templates/transcript/transcript.php?storyId=490948248.

Moore, Hannah. "Why Warhol painted Barbie." British Broadcasting Corporation (BBC). October 1, 2015. https://www.bbc.com/news/magazine-34407991.

Moynihan, Colin. "Frida Kahlo Is a Barbie Doll Now. (Signature Unibrow Not Included.)" *New York Times*. March 9, 2018. https://www.nytimes.com/2018/03/09/arts/design/frida-kahlo-barbie-mattel.html

Nanay, Bence. "Why Is the Barbie Movie so Popular?" *Psychology Today*, Sussex Publishers, 2 Aug. 2023, www.psychologytoday.com/us/blog/psychology-tomorrow/202308/why-is-the-barbie-movie-so-popular.

Nugent, Annabel. "Hot Wheels and Barney: Mattel Plans for Cinematic Universe 'Big as Marvel and DC.'" *The Independent*, Independent Digital News and Media, 31 July 2023, www.independent.co.uk/arts-entertainment/films/news/mattel-barbie-films-polly-pocket-barney-b2384710.html.

Olds, Patrick C. *The Barbie Doll Years: A Comprehensive Listing & Value Guide of Dolls & Accessories*. Collector Books, 2006.

Olson, Elizabeth. "The Ken Doll Turns 50, and Wins a New Face." *New York Times*. March 22, 2011. https://www.nytimes.com/2011/03/22/business/media/22adco.html

Padnani, Amisha. "Sometimes It Is All Just Fun and Games." *New York Times*. May 11, 2017. https://www.nytimes.com/2017/05/11/business/stan-weston-gi-joe-barbie-frisbee-monopoly.html

Rana, Margo. *Collectibly Yours Barbie Doll 1980-1990. Identification & Price Guide*. Hobby House Press Inc., 1998.

Roberts, Ben, and Ian Hart. "Barbie Licensing: Brand Collaborations to Celebrate an Icon." *License Global*, 19 July 2023, www.licenseglobal.com/movies/mattel-announces-licensing-partnerships-ahead-of-barbie-film-.

Rogers, Mary F. *Barbie Culture*. SAGE Publications, 2000.

Rubin, Rebecca. "'Barbie' Surpasses 'The Dark Knight' as Warner Bros.' Highest-Grossing Domestic Release in History." *Variety*, 17 Aug. 2023, variety.com/2023/film/box-office/barbie-warner-bros-biggest-movie-us-beats-dark-knight-1235697702/.

Ruby Lane. "How to Identify a Number One Barbie at the UFDC Doll Museum in Kansas City, Missouri." YouTube. April 2, 2017. https://www.youtube.com/watch?v=RkrK4lNo2pI.

Ruby Lane. "The History of the First Designer of the Barbie Doll: Charlotte Johnson." YouTube. April 14, 2017. https://www.youtube.com/watch?v=WmfWe6jVX9I.

Sarasohn-Kahn, Jane. *Contemporary Barbie Dolls: 1980 And Beyond*. Antique Trader Books, 1997.

Schmid, Cornelius. "6 Holiday Toy Crazes and Why They Captivated Kids (and Parents)." *New York Times*. December 21, 2017. https://www.nytimes.com/2017/12/21/us/christmas-toys.html?

Selin Davis, Lisa. "Like Tomboys and Hate Girlie Girls? That's Sexist." *New York Times*. December 19, 2018. https://www.nytimes.com/2018/12/19/opinion/tomboys-girlie-girls-sexism.html

Shilkitus James, Hillary. *The Complete and Unauthorized Guide to Vintage Barbie Dolls: With Barbie & Skipper Fashions and the Whole Family of Barbie Dolls*. Second Edition. Schiffer Publishing, 2011.

Singer, Natasha. "A Wi-Fi Barbie Doll with the Soul of Siri." *New York Times*. March 29, 2015. https://www.nytimes.com/2015/03/29/technology/a-wi-fi-barbie-doll-with-the-soul-of-siri.html

Singleton, Bridget. *The Art of Barbie*. Vision on, March 2000.

Sink Eames, Sarah. *Barbie Fashion: The Complete History of the Wardrobes of Barbie Doll, Her Friends, and Her Family, Vol. 1: 1959–1967*. Collector Books, 1990.

Spigel, Lynn. *Welcome to the Dreamhouse: Popular Media and Postwar Suburbs*. Duke University Press, 2001

Stewart, James B. "Mattel's Windfall From 'Barbie.'" *New York Times*, 12 Sept 2023, https://www.nytimes.com/2023/09/07/business/barbie-movie-mattel-windfall.html.

St. John Dewein, Sibyl. *The Collector's Encyclopedia of Barbie Dolls and Collectibles*. Collector Books, 1984.

Stone, Tanya Lee. *The Good, the Bad, and the Barbie: A Doll's History and Her Impact on Us*. Viking, 2010.

Supreme, Jpegger. "Stanley Colorite AKA Barbie Man's World Largest Barbie Collection." Jpegy. 2014. http://jpegy.com/geeky/stanley-colorite-aka-barbie-mans-world-largest-barbie-collection-18165.

Thompson, David. "Barbie Movie Box Office: Every Record Broken." *The Direct*, 24 Aug. 2023, thedirect.com/article/barbie-movie-box-office-record.

Tosa, Marco. *Barbie: Four Decades of Fashion, Fantasy, and Fun*. Harry N. Abrams Inc., 1998.

Verbeten, Sharon. *Warman's Barbie Doll Field Guide: Values and Identification*. Krause Publications, 2009.

Vlahos, James. "Barbie Wants to Get to Know Your Child." *New York Times*. September 20, 2015. https://www.nytimes.com/2015/09/20/magazine/barbie-wants-to-get-to-know-your-child.html

Vora, Shivani. "Tour and Hotel News: Barbie in Montreal; Cooking in Chile." *New York Times*. March 9, 2016. https://www.nytimes.com/2016/03/09/travel/tour-and-hotel-news-barbie-in-montreal-cooking-in-chile.html

Witte, Rae. "How Barbie Creator Ruth Handler Changed the Breast Cancer Industry." *Women's Health*, 2 Oct. 2023, www.womenshealthmag.com/health/a44568792/ruth-handler-barbie-creator-breast-cancer-awareness/.

Westenhouser, Kitturah B. *The Story of Barbie*. Collector Books, 1994.

Wichter, Zach. "10 Hot Toys That Changed the Way People Play." *New York Times*. December 9, 2017. https://www.nytimes.com/2017/12/09/business/10-hot-toys-play.html

Zeldis McDonough, Yona. *The Barbie Chronicles: A Living Doll Turns Forty*. Touchstone, 1999.

ABOVE: Mattel's President 2000 Barbie was sold exclusively at Toys "R" Us stores, with a nationwide movement aimed at inspiring and educating young people about their right to vote, and also emphasizing the importance of women in politics. President 2000 Barbie comes dressed in a blue skirt with matching jacket, and also comes with an additional red gown, shown here.

IMAGE CREDITS

Page 2: © Mattel
Page 5: © Mattel
Page 6: © Mattel
Page 8: © Mattel
Page 10-11: © Mattel
Page 12: © Mattel
Page 13: © Mattel
Page 14: © Mattel
Page 15: © Mattel
Page 16: © Mattel
Page 17: © Mattel
Page 18: © Found Image Holdings/Getty Images
Page 20: © Mattel
Page 21: © Mattel
Page 22: © Mattel
Page 23: © SSPL/Getty Images
Page 24: © Mattel
Page 25: © Sueddeutsche Zeitung Photo/Alamy Stock Photo
Page 27: © Mattel
Page 28: © Mattel
Page 29: © Mattel
Page 30-31: © Tony Korody/Getty Images
Page 31: © Mattel
Page 32: © Don Bartletti/Getty Images
Page 34: (Top) © CBS Photo Archive/Getty Images; (Bottom) © Larry Ellis/Stringer via Getty Images
Page 35: © Mattel
Page 36: © Mattel
Page 37: © Mattel
Page 38: © Mattel
Page 39: © Mattel
Page 40: © Mattel
Page 41: © Mattel
Page 42: © Courtesy of Bradley Justice
Page 43: © Mattel
Page 44: © Courtesy of Bradley Justice
Page 45: © Courtesy of Bradley Justice
Page 46: © Mattel
Page 47: (Top) © Keystone-France/Getty Images; (Bottom) © Mattel
Page 48: © Mattel
Page 49: © Mattel
Page 50: © Courtesy of Bradley Justice
Page 51: © Courtesy of Bradley Justice
Page 52-53: © ullstein bild Dtl./Getty Images
Page 54: © Keystone-France/Getty Images
Page 56: © Mattel
Page 57: © Mattel
Page 58: © Mattel
Page 59: © Mattel
Page 60-61: © Mattel

Page 62: © Mattel
Page 63: © Mattel
Page 64: © Mattel
Page 65: © David M. Benett/Getty Images
Page 66: © Mattel
Page 67: © Mattel
Page 68-69: © Mattel
Page 69: © Mattel
Page 70: © Mattel
Page 72: © Mattel
Page 73: © Mattel
Page 74: © Mattel
Page 75: © Mattel
Page 76: © Mattel
Page 77: © Mattel
Page 78: © Mattel
Page 79: © Mattel
Page 80: © Mattel
Page 81: © Mattel
Page 82: © Mattel
Page 84-85: © Mattel
Page 86: © Mattel
Page 88: © Mattel
Page 89: © Mattel
Page 90: © Mattel
Page 91: © Peter Bischoff/Stringer via Getty Images
Page 92: © Mattel
Page 93: © Mattel
Page 94-95: © Mattel
Page 96: © Pierre Vauthey/Getty Images
Page 98: © Luci Nicholson/Stringer via Getty Images
Page 99: © Mattel
Page 100: (Top) © Daniel Simon/Getty Images; (Bottom) © Bruce Glikas/Getty Images
Page 101: © Michael Tran/Getty Images
Page 102: © Johnny Green-PA Images via Getty Images
Page 103: (Left) ©PA Images/Alamy Stock Photo; (Right) © Mattel
Page 104: © Cassy Cohen/Getty Images
Page 105: © Gilles Bassignac/Getty Images
Page 106: © Gilles Bassignac/Getty Images
Page 107: © Stuart C. Wilson/Getty Images
Page 108: (Top) © Lawrence Lucier/Stringer via Getty Images; (Bottom) © Timur Emek/Getty Images
Page 109: (Top) © Time & Life Pictures/Getty Images; (Bottom) © Venturelli/Getty Images
Page 110: © Mattel
Page 111: © Mattel
Page 112: © Stephen Chernin/Getty Images
Page 113: © DMI/Getty Images
Page 114: © Frazer Harrison/Getty Images
Page 115: © Thierry Chesnot/Getty Images

Page 116: (Left) © Scott Gries/Getty Images; (Right) © Getty Images
Page 117: (Top) © Mirrorpix/Getty Images; (Bottom) © Pascal Le Segretain/Getty Images
Page 118: © Mattel
Page 119: © Mattel
Page 120: Photos by Robert Ryan/Courtesy of Corazon Ugalde Yellen Armenta
Page 121: © Matthew Fearn-PA Images via Getty Images
Page 122: © Robin Marchant/Getty Images
Page 123: © Michael Crabtree-PA Images via Getty Images
Page 124: © The AGE/Getty Images
Page 125: © The AGE/Getty Images
Page 126-127: © Jean Baptiste Lacroix/Getty Images
Page 128: © Lawrence Lucier/Stringer via Getty Images
Page 130: © Chesnot/Getty Images
Page 131: Courtesy of Jian Yang
Page 132: Courtesy of Jian Yang
Page 133: Courtesy of Jian Yang
Page 134: © Kevin Winter/Getty Images
Page 135: © Paolo Bona/Shutterstock
Page 136: © chrisdorney/Shutterstock
Page 137: © Courtesy of Grace Mulgrew from Grace's World
Page 138: © Mattel
Page 139: © Mattel
Page 140: © Barcroft Media/Getty Images
Page 141: © Barcroft Media/Getty Images
Page 142-143: © Alexander Tamargo/Getty Images
Page 144: © Robert Mora Getty Images
Page 146: © Hector Mata/Getty Images
Page 147: (Top) © Courtesy of Kitturah Westenhouser; (Bottom) © Don Bartletti/Getty Images
Page 148: © picture alliance/Getty Images
Page 149: © picture alliance/Getty Images
Page 150-151: © Chesnot/Getty Images
Page 152: © Mattel
Page 154: © Warner Brothers
Page 156: © Spirit Halloween
Page 157: © Mattel
Page 158: © Mattel
Page 159: © Mattel
Page 160-168: © Mattel
Page 169: (Top left) © Warner Brothers; (Bottom center) © JOCA_PH/Shutterstock.com; (Top right, Bottom left, Bottom right) © Mattel
Page 170: © Mattel
Page 171: © Mattel
Page 174 © Yvonne Hemsey/Getty Images
Page 176: Courtesy of Robin Gerber

ACKNOWLEDGMENTS

Many thanks to my smart, patient, and enthusiastic editor Bonnie Honeycutt. She guided this book with skill and good humor.

The stellar staff at the Barbie Brand were a joy to interview, and showed enormous generosity in answering questions, explaining the intricacies and evolution of the brand, and in sharing their personal stories. Particular thanks to: Lisa McKnight, Kim Culmone, Michelle Chidoni, Robert Best, Matt Repicky, and Liz Maglione. This book was also greatly enriched by help from Bill Greening, Brand Historian, and Eliana Ruiz, Archivist, who continue to do important work in archiving the documentary and visual history of Barbie. Their help was invaluable.

Special thanks to Kitturah Westenhouser, who shared her tape recordings of Ruth Handler from the early 1990s, and whose *The Story of Barbie* (1994 and 1999 editions) remains a treasure trove of information and historical photographs. Thanks also to Bradley Justice, who has done amazing work in unearthing the story of Charlotte Johnson, and who helped with many questions I had along the way. Every interviewee shared their love of all things Barbie with passion and clarity. Thank you all!

Finally, my husband, Tony Records, gave the kind of support, good humor, and love that I've been privileged to enjoy for thirty plus years. If I'm lucky, we'll get another thirty years, like Ruth and Elliot Handler!

ABOUT THE AUTHOR

Robin Gerber is a best-selling author and historian. She is the author of *Leadership the Eleanor Roosevelt Way: Timeless Strategies from the First Lady of Courage*. Her most recent book is the first biography of the founder of Mattel, Ruth Handler, titled *Barbie and Ruth: The Story of the World's Most Famous Doll and the Woman Who Created Her*. Her articles have appeared in *USA Today*, the *Washington Post*, *The Philadelphia Inquirer*, and numerous other newspapers and magazines. Prior to becoming an author, Robin practiced law in Washington, D.C., and worked on Capitol Hill. She has studied and written about leadership development since 1975.